Bear
Awareness

Bear Awareness

Questions and Answers on Taming Your Wild Mind

AJAHN BRAHM

Wisdom Publications
199 Elm Street
Somerville, MA 02144 USA
wisdompubs.org

Library of Congress Cataloging-in-Publication Data
Names: Ajahn Brahm, 1951– author.
Title: Bear awareness: questions and answers on taming your wild mind / Ajahn Brahm.
Description: Somerville, MA: Wisdom Publications, [2017] |
Identifiers: LCCN 2017018046 (print) | LCCN 2017033648 (ebook) | ISBN 9781614292715 (ebook) | ISBN 161429271X (ebook) | ISBN 9781614292562 (pbk.: alk. paper) | ISBN 1614292566 (pbk.: alk. paper)
Subjects: LCSH: Meditation—Buddhism—Miscellanea. | Thought and thinking—Religious aspects—Buddhism—Miscellanea. | Buddhism—Miscellanea.
Classification: LCC BQ5612 (ebook) | LCC BQ5612 .A33 2017 (print) | DDC 294.3/4435—dc23
LC record available at https://lccn.loc.gov/2017018046

ISBN 978-1-61429-256-2 ebook ISBN 978-1-61429-271-5

21 20 19 18 17
5 4 3 2 1

Cover design by Phil Pascuzzo. Interior design by James D. Skatges.
Set in Diacritical Garamond Pro 11.5/14.

Wisdom Publications' books are printed on acid-free paper and meet the guidelines for permanence and durability of the Production Guidelines for Book Longevity of the Council on Library Resources.

♻ This book was produced with environmental mindfulness.
For more information, please visit wisdompubs.org/wisdom-environment.

Printed in the United States of America.

Please visit fscus.org.

Contents

Preface

Asking questions is good *kamma*. In the *Shorter Exposition of Kamma Sutta* (MN 135), a student asked the Buddha why some people are wealthy but others have to work their butts off and still struggle to get by. The Buddha answered that it is because of kamma from a past life. Those who were stingy in their previous life are likely to be poor in this one.

The Buddha was also asked why some people are good looking while others are so ugly that even a makeover at an expensive salon fails to make them attractive. The Buddha answered that the kammic cause of ugliness in this life is having been angry and irritable in the previous one.

Then the Buddha was asked what the kammic cause for stupidity in this life is. Why do some people have to study so hard at school, even hiring private tutors, and still struggle to get passing grades, whereas others seem to do little work and get straight A's? The Buddha answered—and this is very important in order for you to understand the purpose of this book—that the kammic cause for being a dummy in your next life is . . . NOT ASKING QUESTIONS IN THIS LIFE.

So thanks to all the future geniuses who asked the questions for this book. You will all have such an easy time at school in your next life!

AJAHN BRAHM
Perth, Australia

A Note from the Editors

Ajahn Brahm is known and appreciated not only for the content of his teachings but also for his style of delivery and his sense of humor. His "bad" jokes lift the mood and open the heart to a kinder and more compassionate perspective. Often the truth of what he says is in the joke. But the main purpose in looking on the bright side is to release problems that are keeping us from moving forward on the Buddhist path.

This book was originally conceived to commemorate Ajahn Brahm's fortieth anniversary as a monk. It draws together questions and answers from recent retreats led by Ajahn Brahm at Jhana Grove Retreat Centre in Australia. At the end of each day, retreatants were invited to write down their questions and place them anonymously in a small basket. Ajahn Brahm would then read out each question in front of the assembled meditators before giving his response. Fans of Ajahn Brahm's previous books will recognize some of the stories here, but the intimacy of the question-and-answer format provides a fresh experience of learning from a master meditator.

In any book presenting the Buddha's Dhamma, the teachings are clearly the central concern, but there is more to these questions than just the spoken word. In compiling and editing the text, we became aware that much of the beautiful atmosphere at Jhana Grove, the shared affection and humor among the community, and even subtler nuances taking place in a group Q & A forum, are not conveyed in words alone. In the evening assemblies, as the sun set, its colored light streaming through the eucalyptus, one could hear the distant, cackling laughter of the kookaburra. The stillness of the Australian bush was matched by the stillness of the listeners. Such a stillness of mind can benefit readers as well, enhancing the experience of this book, so we urge you to imagine you are there in the hall with Ajahn Brahm, that you have spent the day in meditation, and that he is addressing you personally.

For those not well acquainted with the many Pali-language terms that permeate the study of Theravada Buddhism, non-English words, as well as names, are explained at the end of the book.

1.

The Hahayana Approach to Meditation

Why it's a good idea to lighten up.

What's *mettā*? I'm just a beginner.

That's such a wonderful question. Whoever wrote that question is so kind and lovely. You must be close to enlightenment.

The way I'm treating you is called *mettā*. Mettā is "loving-kindness"—it's care, it's compassion, it's acceptance, it's respect. When you have mettā toward someone, you respect him, you're kind to her, you give him the benefit of the doubt—even when he snores loudly in the middle of the night. If you have loving-kindness toward other people, they're no longer a problem. With loving-kindness toward yourself, you're no longer a problem to yourself. And when you have loving-kindness toward every moment, beautiful mettā to this moment, you're on the highway to enlightenment. The path becomes so easy.

One reason people don't feel peace is that they're not kind enough to their minds. With mettā you give yourself a break—you don't force yourself. You look upon your body and mind as good friends, and you then work together in a kind and compassionate way.

In my book *Who Ordered This Truckload of Dung?* I explained that mettā is the ability to open the door of your heart no matter what you're experiencing, no matter what's happening. It's beautiful, unconditional goodwill. For example, you may have been lazy, and perhaps you think you need to be punished. That's not mettā. Be kind to yourself even when you've been lazy or slack or have, say, broken retreat precepts in the afternoon by munching on some cookies. Whatever you've been up to, give yourself a break. And as for other people, it doesn't matter if they've been making all sorts of disturbing noises while you're trying to meditate: "May they have happiness and well-being also."

This beautiful sense of mettā does not depend on what people have done or what you've done. Give mettā to every moment. Be kind to yourself in every moment, no matter what the moment is like and how you're experiencing it—whether you're dull, restless, or frustrated. In other words, wish every moment well.

How do I increase mettā?

Mettā meditation is a way of deliberately generating goodwill toward all beings. We learn how to recognize it and how to develop it further. In mettā meditation people usually say a few words to themselves over and over again: "May all beings be happy and well. May all beings be free from suffering. May I be happy. May I be at peace." But you can use whatever words you like. The important thing is to pay attention to the spaces between the words. Say, "May I be happy and well," and then pause to give the words a chance to work.

You will find that the words have power. If you pause to connect to that power, you'll understand the true meaning of "May all beings be free from suffering," and the mind will start to generate mettā. The words just light the match that ignites the mettā. The feelings that come after the words, that's mettā. It's incredibly pleasant.

Repeat the words only until you feel the mettā. Every time you give an instruction to your mind, your mind starts looking in that direction. The words point the mind toward mettā. When your mind is full of mettā, you no longer need the words. You've followed the signposts and reached the destination—you're at mettā. If you really cultivate that feeling—become familiar and at ease with it—it becomes very powerful. You can take it all the way into profound meditative states.

So ride the words until you feel them. What if I say, "Peace . . . peace . . . peace . . ."? Do you feel any peace? Do you experience its meaning? Once you get your head around what it means, once you have peace in your mind, you no longer need to say the word. Only when the experience fades do you say the word again. Keep on saying it until there's no need, until you have peace.

This is how we practice loving-kindness. We use the words to generate an emotion, and when that emotion is strong, we turn toward the emotion and let go of the words. The words have done their job. If you wish, you can visualize it like a golden light in your heart. Sometimes visualization helps.

Once it gets to a certain point, it's self-sustaining. You don't need to say anything anymore; you just feel mettā—you *are* mettā—and it extends to all beings. If you develop the mettā even further, you'll get so much happiness and joy, so much *pīti-sukha*, that a beautiful light appears in the mind—a *nimitta*. You're just sitting there, blissing out. A proper mettā nimitta is beautiful, lovely, and easy to focus on, and it takes you into the absorptions, the *jhānas*. I kept repeating these words of the Buddha to the monks during one three-month retreat: *Sukhino cittaṁ samādhiyati*—"From happiness, from bliss, the mind becomes very still." From the bliss and happiness of mettā, the mind gets incredibly still, and then nimittas and jhānas just happen.

So feel the resonance after you say, "May all beings be happy and well." Keep on saying the words (and really mean them!), and dwell on those feelings until they get very, very strong and self-sustaining. It's just like when you're lighting a fire and you need to strike the match several times. But once the fire gets going, it just takes off. That's mettā meditation, and it's very powerful.

One of my favorite mettā stories is about one of the famous Thai forest monks. He was wandering through the jungle one afternoon when he arrived at a certain village. He announced to the headman that he was going to stay there for the night. The headman was very pleased to have a forest monk there. He arranged for the villagers to come out to listen to the monk give a Dhamma talk that evening and then feed him the following morning.

And what did the monk do for two hours until the evening talk? He sat down under a tree to meditate. But after a couple of minutes, he realized that he was sitting under the wrong tree: a big ants' nest was close by. The first ant crawled up his foot and then up his leg and bit him. Ouch! And then a second, a third, a tenth, and a twentieth, all biting him! He was a tough monk, so he just sat there.

Before he knew it, however, he was standing up and running away. But he caught himself, stopped, and thought: "I'm a forest monk. I shouldn't be running away like this."

He turned around. The spot where he had been sitting was swarming with thousands of red ants. He decided he was going to sit right in the middle of them. (They don't make monks like that these days!) As he sat, the ants started to crawl up and bite him again, but this time he changed the object of his meditation from the breath to mettā: "May all beings be happy and well, especially these red ants. If you are really hungry, try my arms and knock yourself out!" (He didn't really say that—I made that up.) After he had done mettā meditation for a couple of minutes, the ants stopped biting him. They were still crawling over and irritating him, but they had stopped biting. After another few minutes he had an amazing sensation: Instead of the ants crawling up, they were crawling down, until the last ant crawled off his foot. All he had done was to give loving-kindness to all beings. It was a wonderfully deep meditation.

After two hours had passed he heard the villagers coming. They were making strange noises, as if they were dancing. He thought, "What a strange custom they have in this village—when they come to visit a monk they dance on the way!" But then he realized why they were dancing—they were being bitten by the red ants! The area all around was carpeted with red ants except for a one-meter circle around him, which was like a no-man's land. He realized that the red ants were protecting him!

That's how powerful loving-kindness, or mettā, meditation is. The animals look after you and protect you.

Can you send mettā magic to the dishwasher? The one here has stopped working.

Why do you need the dishwasher? You've got two hands! You've got a sponge. People these days have got all these electronic things and just have to press buttons. It's wonderful when things go wrong. It means you get a chance to make good kamma. This is actually a deep teaching.

When you volunteer—it's not your job, you just want to help others—it's amazing how much joy you get.

One of my seminal experiences as a young monk took place in northeast Thailand just before the ordination of three novices. When you ordained as a monk, you had to make your own set of three robes, starting with plain white pieces of cloth. It took about two or three days. You had to sew them together and then dye them with jackfruit dye. To do this you had to haul water from the well and gather wood to start a fire. You had to get branches from a jackfruit tree, chop them up into little chips, boil those chips to extract the dye, concentrate the dye, and then use that to dye the cloth brown. It was hard work.

The three novices were in the process of making their robes. They hadn't slept for ages, because to make the dye you had to keep the fire going and keep working. After the evening chanting I went to the dyeing shed. Seeing that the poor novices were very tired, I said: "Look, you go and have a few hours' sleep. I'll stay up tonight to look after your dyeing. But don't tell anybody, because it's breaking the rules." They went off to bed, and I looked after the dye pot all night. At three o'clock in the morning the bell rang. The three novices came out and carried on with the dyeing while I went to the morning chanting and meditation. I was bright and clear and wasn't sleepy at all. I was full of energy!

Later, when we were on almsround, I said to the senior monk: "This is really strange. I haven't slept all night, but I have all this wonderful energy, and I am not at all tired. I haven't the slightest trace of sloth and torpor. Why is that?"

"It's because you've made good kamma, because you've helped others," he said. "You've sacrificed your sleep for others. The result is that you get special energy."

I've made use of this lesson throughout my monastic life. Any opportunity I have for doing good kamma, even though I don't need to, even though I'm a senior monk, I'll take it. Why? Because of the joy and energy I get from it.

So it doesn't matter whose turn it is to wash the dishes: "Get out of the way, I'm going to do it!"

Compared with just doing your duties, it's much more fun when you want to give, when you want to help, and you get much more energy that way. So it's a great blessing when the dishwasher breaks down. It gives you more opportunity to make merit, to make good kamma. Brilliant!

Beauty and the Breath

Can you please explain how to make the breath beautiful, how to get to that sustained attention on the breath that is natural and imbued with peace?

To achieve a beautiful, sustained attention on the breath, try to incline toward the beautiful. When you go outside, look at the beautiful flowers, not at the spiders. Look at the beautiful sky, but don't feel the cold. Whatever it is, just incline toward the beauty in life. There are problems and difficulties in life, but instead of looking at that, look at the opposite.

For instance, even if you're sick with cancer, the cancer is only one part of the body; the rest is all right. Or you may have a motorcycle accident and lose a leg, but you've got another leg. That's called a spare! Whatever happens in life, there are always good things to focus on. Beauty is always there if you look for it.

However, some people are so negative that they can find faults in anything. For them even a beautiful retreat center sucks. The afternoons are too hot; the cushions are too hard. If there's no schedule, they want more structure. If there's a schedule, oh, it's too strict! Regardless of what happens, they can always find something to complain about. If you look at things that way, you'll never get to the beautiful breath.

Instead, say you are in retreat: think how wonderful it is just to be there, to watch the breath and have nothing else to do in the whole world. If you've got nothing to do except be with this body and mind, isn't that bliss? When you think like that, the perception of the beautiful arises naturally throughout the day, and then it's easy to get to the beautiful breath.

After a short time of meditation my breath became very quiet and effortless. It remained like this for two or three hours. Please enlighten me on this.

Stay like that for another couple of hours, and you'll enlighten yourself! Watching the breath effortlessly and peacefully for two to three hours is exactly what's supposed to happen.

How many things should we watch in an in-breath and out-breath? Should we watch the beginning, the middle, and the end of the breath—and the space in between the in-breath and the out-breath, as well as the space in between the out-breath and the in-breath?

The breath is continuous and so is watching it. You don't just watch the beginning, the middle, and the end of the breath—that's only three spots. There are probably thousands of spots to watch for each breath. Close your eyes and just watch one breath. See how many sensations you can notice. There are heaps of them! Little by little, you learn to see more and more of each breath. Eventually you see the whole lot without any interruption, right from the beginning all the way to the end. That's what we're supposed to watch.

All things follow from the stillness of the mind, and the way to keep the mind still is by observing the breath. Most of the time we think, because we're not really happy. Thinking usually comes from discontent. If you're really happy and at peace and everything is OK, you don't want to be distracted by thinking. Why would you want to spoil your happiness by thinking? When you're really happy, thinking just disappears. And that's how the mind gets still.

Sound is the last thing to disappear as your meditation deepens, so don't be discouraged if, say, you're doing a group meditation and you hear coughs and sneezes even though you feel calm and your attention on your breath is beautiful. As your meditation progresses, you will experience the coughs and sneezes as being a long way away. You will hear the sounds but as if they're a hundred miles away. Eventually they will disappear, and you don't want to get out of that state.

Walk This Way

If I am uncomfortable doing breath meditation, should I learn walking meditation? Can you explain how walking meditation is done?

Walking meditation can be an alternative to breath meditation. There are so many places where you can do walking meditation. At the retreat center we've got walking paths, or you can go out into the forest. Choose a path that is neither too long nor too short. Use a straight path, not a circular one.

Walk naturally. Start at the beginning of the path and put your gaze six feet in front of you (roughly—you don't need to get a tape measure). In this way you can see what's ahead of you and feel quite safe that you're not going to walk over a cliff or tread on anything. Then you just walk.

As you're walking, don't think about the future or the past—stop all this thinking business. Don't be concerned about the stock market or the football or about what's happening at home. Instead, put your full awareness on the feelings in your feet and legs as they move. Know the left foot as it moves. Know the right foot.

First of all, get into the present moment. Secondly, be silent. Thirdly, put your attention on whichever foot is moving. Fourthly, bring full awareness to all of the walking, which means from the very beginning of the left foot moving to the very end of the left foot moving, and then from the very beginning of the right foot moving to the very end of the right foot moving.

What part of the foot leaves the ground first? What part leaves the ground last? Once the foot leaves the ground, does it go straight up? Does it go forward a bit? How does it move through the air? Feel all the sensations that tell you what your foot is doing. What part meets the ground first? What's that sensation like? Feel it as fully as possible. What's the last part of your foot that meets the ground? Then feel the weight of your body as it transfers onto that foot. Just walking, you experience all these wonderful sensations.

Don't try to force your gait—just walk naturally. Be like a passenger observing all the amazing feelings in your legs as they carry you along. When you get to the end of the path, stop and feel all the sensations of turning around.

The benefit of focusing on the feelings in the body is that you can't think too much about them. You can't have much of a conversation about the feeling in the foot when it meets the ground. It keeps you in the present moment. After a while you get very still and peaceful because the feelings become delightful and absorb your attention.

Another advantage of walking meditation is that you don't have to worry about an aching knee or back, which often happens while sitting. You're moving, and it's very comfortable for your body. Do it as long as you feel happy. Get as peaceful and go as deep as you possibly can. You can get very peaceful in walking meditation.

These are very simple instructions. Nothing in meditation is complicated.

Some people prefer walking to sitting meditation. That's one reason we have three big walking meditation halls at the retreat center—to encourage it. So experiment with walking meditation. Sometimes when you get peaceful in walking meditation, it enhances your sitting meditation—it gets much deeper. So make use of it.

When I reach the wall in my walking meditation, I feel disrupted and experience a break in the smooth walking. How can I overcome this? Surely I can't walk through the wall yet!

How do you know you can't walk through a wall? Don't just follow beliefs—give it a try! If you really want to, you can walk a marathon's distance. You don't have to stop. That way you won't be disturbed!

The reason it's good to turn around in walking meditation is that sometimes you lose your mindfulness—you start to fantasize, to dream, to plan, or whatever. Walking on a short path makes you stop and turn around quite frequently, which brings you back to the present moment.

I also like the *idea* of turning around and coming back: You end up where you started, and that's a good metaphor for life. We always think we're getting somewhere. But where do we really get? Most of the time we just get back to where we started. How many times have you gone on retreat, said goodbye to your new friends, and then gone home? This is what happens. Things just go round and round in the circles of life.

You can also do walking meditation with a mantra. It's fun and it can give you great insight. I learned this mantra in Thailand many years ago. When you're walking on the path, as the left foot moves forward, you silently say, "I will die," and as the other foot moves forward, "That's for sure." "I will die . . . that's for sure."

When people start that, they sometimes think it's a joke. After a while, they realize it's not a joke. This is one thing that is so true you can't deny it. You may get frightened: "My God, it's true!" Keep on walking, and keep on saying "I will die, that's for sure." Eventually you get through the fear, and because you know it's true, all your attachments and all your worries—about emails, your business, your spouse, your kids, even your health—all of them just vanish.

Since it is true that "I will die, that's for sure," what am I worrying about all this other stuff for? You get really peaceful. And you get some very deep insights in how to be free. "I will die, that's for sure." What a relief! Walking meditation creates a deep sense of stillness, happiness, and insight.

When I was in Malaysia once, people were getting a bit bored with just sitting down and watching their breath or doing walking meditation. I said that in Buddhism we sometimes have to adapt to the country we're in, and so I encouraged people to do the Australian walking meditation method, which is inspired by the kangaroos. I explained that you start at one end of the path, curl your hands like the paws of a kangaroo . . . and hop, which I also demonstrated, much to their amusement. When you get to the other end, you turn around and hop back. It's Australian walking meditation! Try it. At the very least it will make anyone watching you burst out laughing, and it will make you happy too! That will make meditation less serious—we can have some fun.

By Any Means Necessary

In one of your books you mention watching a wall. When we're bored watching the inside of our eyes, can we watch a wall instead? And what are we supposed to do if the wall disappears?

Yes, often we begin meditation by closing our eyes, but you can watch a wall if you like. But to get the wall to disappear, your mind has to be pretty still, without thoughts. A lot of the time people watch the wall with only 10 percent of their attention, while 90 percent is given to fantasizing and dreaming—thinking about dinner, remembering the past, remembering a favorite movie. If your mind isn't still and most of your attention is elsewhere, the wall doesn't disappear. Only when your mind is still will the wall vanish. It's weird when it happens. You can try it, but it's much better to watch your body disappear.

Is it OK to meditate wearing noise-canceling headphones or earplugs? I live on a somewhat noisy street.

I can't see why not. You can wear big headphones or just noise-canceling ones. You can use an iPod to play "I will die, that's for sure" right into your ears! Make it interesting.

Don't get caught up in what you think meditation looks like. You don't have to be able to sit in perfect lotus to have a good meditation—the Buddha didn't always. There are statues of the Buddha sitting in chairs, and many monks meditate in chairs. Ajahn Sujato normally meditates in a chair because he's got very bad knees. When I'm on an aircraft, I meditate in a chair. If I ask if I can sit in the aisle to meditate, they won't let me, so I have to do it in the chair.

Please explain how to meditate when you are in pain. How do you concentrate on the source of the pain?

If you're uncomfortable sitting on the floor but really want to sit on the floor, do yoga or stretching exercises. Otherwise, sit in a chair if you have to. Or lie down on your bed if need be. It's just stupid to subject yourself to pain unnecessarily. And if you're in great pain regardless of your sitting position, take a pain killer! Really. Pain is distracting. But sometimes pain will not go away whether you sit in a chair or on the ground or lie down on your bed—even if you take a pain killer.

One way of overcoming such pain is to put your attention in the center of it—which is a tough thing to do—and then do relaxation with compassion. At the very least you'll relax a few tense muscles, which is likely to be part of the problem. Some pains are just the body overreacting to an infection or a wound. By relaxing, you're overcoming that overreaction.

I know this because I sometimes suffer from hay fever. It's just an overreaction to a tiny bit of pollen. When I focus my mind on my nose and relax that area, it does help quite considerably.

Another way of dealing with pain is by using mindfulness with insight. This technique is based on the fact that intense pain is normally confined to a small area of the body. Imagine drawing a box around the pain—the pain is inside and the rest of your body is outside. Then use your imagination to expand that box. As you're expanding the box, you're expanding the pain. Instead of making the pain worse, this actually dilutes it. Expand it to twice its size in all directions—twice the width, twice the height, twice the depth. Can you see that if you use your imagination in this way it actually helps to relax the pain? Contraction creates more pain; expansion tends to alleviate it. If that doesn't work, try the Buddha's simile, retold in my book *Who Ordered This*

Truckload of Dung? about the monster that came into the emperor's palace (SN 11:22).

A demon came into the emperor's palace and sat down on the emperor's throne, and everyone said: "Get out of here! You don't belong! Who do you think you are?!"

And the demon grew bigger, uglier, smellier, and more offensive. How do you get rid of a demon? Not with anger.

Then the emperor returned and said: "Welcome, demon. Thank you for coming to visit me. Please, can I get you something to eat?"

With every act of kindness it became smaller, less ugly, less smelly, and less offensive. The problem grew smaller and smaller until a last act of kindness made it vanish completely.

That's a wonderful teaching of the Buddha's. We call that an anger-eating demon, one that feeds on anger and ill will. The more anger and ill will you give it, the worse it gets. Pain is a classic example of an anger-eating demon. If you have pain in the body and say, "Get out of here, you don't belong," it gets worse. But if you're kind to the pain—"Welcome! I will look after you"—the pain diminishes. Every act of kindness, every moment of unconditionally opening the door of your heart, relaxes and reduces the pain.

A lot of energy builds up in my head and around my eyes. Should I continue meditating? How do I get rid of the pressure?

You don't need to get rid of anything. Let the energy build up. Whatever it's doing, it's probably doing it for a good purpose. As long as you're nice and peaceful and the meditation is going well, it's probably just healing going on. If you have hot spots in your body when you're meditating, it's because your body knows it needs energy there.

A woman came to me during a retreat complaining that her shoulders and neck were so hot, it was almost like a fever.

She said, "What's going on? It's weird."

I said, "When did you have your whiplash?"

She said, "I never told you that, Ajahn Brahm. You've got psychic powers! You know my past!"

I said, "No, I was just adding one and one and getting two."

It was obvious. When you have a hot spot, it means there's an injury there that's healing. And the most common injury to the neck and shoulders is whiplash from a car accident. I surmised that she must have had that injury a while ago, but now that she was letting go and getting out of the way, her body was able to heal itself. She was freeing the energy channels, and the energy could go where it was needed.

She felt really good afterward. She said that she'd never been so relaxed since the accident.

As long as you're nice and peaceful and the meditation is going well, if you have hot spots or energy building up in your body, it's probably just healing going on—your body needs energy there. So if that's what you have, excellent. Just carry on and let go.

What Russian Dolls Have To Do with It

What's your opinion on using *kasiṇas* instead of the breath as an object of meditation?

A *nimitta* is a mental object, and because the visual sense predominates for most people, it's natural for most to perceive the nimitta as a light. It's possible to have feeling nimittas, but they can easily deceive you. They could just be normal feelings in the mind. So be careful with the feeling nimittas. To be sure you have a real nimitta, it's much better to develop the perception of a light. Most meditation traditions use the light nimitta. Don't try to find a shortcut.

Using a *kasiṇa* (a visualized colored disk) is one way of generating a nimitta. It is usually much more difficult to focus on than the breath, unless you have a very visual mind. If you can visualize things clearly, like an artist who can draw and paint, then kasiṇas may be useful for you.

It's very rare for people to teach the kasiṇas. The basic idea is to visualize a colored disk so clearly that whether your eyes are open or closed it appears just the same. Not many people can do that.

How long should you watch a nimitta?

A nimitta lasts for just a moment. That's all there ever is. Remember that if you're thinking of how long, you've lost the present moment; you're caught up in time again, you're measuring, and you've lost the plot. Watch the nimitta for one moment, the moment called "now."

A real nimitta is so bright that you won't feel your body anymore, and you won't know what you're doing. If you're walking outside, you'll keep walking, walking, walking, and we might have to go deep into the forest to find you! All you're seeing is this bright light—you might end up in the ocean! A proper nimitta is so bright that you lose all awareness of the body. If you do see a nimitta, just sit down and close your eyes. In this way you'll go even deeper.

If the nimitta disappears and you go into jhāna, you haven't got any choice but to carry on enjoying yourself. It should be fun. The second jhāna is within the first one, right in the center of it. This means that you always have to go through the first jhāna to get to the second. And to get the third one, you have to go through the second, because the third jhāna is right in the center of the second one. And the fourth one is right in the center of the third. You always go in . . . in . . . in. That's an important point about meditation: You never go *on* to the next stage but always deeper *in*.

Think of Russian dolls: One is inside another, which in turn is inside another, which in turn is inside another. That's meditation. You start off with the mind. Inside the mind, with all of its thinking about the past and future, you find the present moment. In the center of the present moment, you find silence. In the center of the silence, you find the breath. In the center of the breath, you find the full awareness of the breath. In the middle of the full awareness of the breath, you find the delightful breath. In the middle of the delightful breath comes the nimitta. In the middle of the nimitta, you get the first jhāna. You then go through all the jhānas. Finally, in the center of the fourth immaterial attainment, you find the end of everything. This is the jewel in the heart of the lotus.

Do you know what's there? Would you believe me if I told you? If you did, you'd be gullible! How can you know that what I'm saying is correct? Anyone who believes simply because they're told is stupid. So don't believe what I'm saying. And if you don't believe me, what's the point of my telling you?

Well, there's nothing there.

THE GOOD, THE BAD, AND VIPASSANĀ

You've taught us how to meditate by visualizing our good actions, our good speech, and so on. It's all about ourselves.

It's hard to visualize other people's stuff. Yes, you can fantasize about it, but you don't really know it. All you've got to work on is your own stuff. So work on that first of all, especially the good things. With the bad things, just assume it wasn't you.

There was once a Sufi teacher who, at the end of a retreat, took his students to a fair. At one booth, a teddy bear was the prize for hitting a target with an arrow. The teacher said: "I'm a good archer. I know how to use a bow." So he paid for three arrows.

He loaded the first arrow and quickly released it. It went only halfway to the target.

His students raised their eyebrows, saying, "Have you ever used a bow before?"

"That was the shot of a hasty man," he said.

He loaded the next arrow. Pulling the bow back farther and steadying himself, he shot again. It went about a mile to the side of the target and nearly killed someone!

The students said: "Give up! People are laughing at you. You're a well-known teacher—you'll ruin your reputation."

"No, no," he said. "That was the shot of a proud man."

And so came the third arrow. The students started to walk away, muttering, "You don't know how to use a bow." But then, of course, the third arrow went straight through the middle of the target.

As the teacher was collecting his teddy bear, the students asked him, "If the first shot was that of a hasty man, and the second that of a proud man, whose shot was the third one?"

And he said, "Oh, that was me."

Some days you're not in your right mind, a bit grumpy, not feeling too good, a bit off your game. Whenever things aren't quite right or you make mistakes, pass it over. But whenever you do something successful, take that as the real you. Why not? That's letting go of the failures of the past and retaining the happiness.

You learn much more from happiness and success than from mistakes. If you keep on focusing on the happiness, on the goodness, on your successes, you tend to learn the secret of happiness and success. This means you repeat it. On the other hand, people who keep on thinking about their mistakes and try to analyze their failed meditations get depressed. You're reinforcing your failures instead of just letting them go. You may think you're going to learn from your mistakes, but instead you just get upset, depressed, and angry. However, if you remember your successes, what worked, and why you were happy, then you learn the secret of happiness. It's not what we've got but how we work with it.

I get confused by the names of different meditation techniques. What are *ānāpānasati*, *vipassanā*, and *samatha*?

Ānāpānasati is "breath meditation," *vipassanā* is "insight," and *samatha* is "calm." But there's no difference between them—they're all the same. Here's a story I tell on every retreat.

Once there was a married couple. The guy's name was Sam (samatha), and his wife was called Vi (vipassanā). After lunch one day Sam and Vi decided to go for a walk up Meditation Mountain with their two dogs. One dog was called Mettā and the other dog was called Ānāpāna (ānāpānasati).

Sam wanted to go to the top because it was so peaceful there, and he just loved the stillness. Vi went up for the view. She took her new camera, which could take incredible insight shots over great distances. Mettā went because it's good fun walking up Meditation Mountain. And Ānāpāna went for a breath of fresh air.

Halfway up it started to become peaceful and still, and Sam was delighted. But because he had eyes, he also enjoyed the view. Vi was already snapping photos because she could see so far. But she was also enjoying the peace. Mettā was wagging her tail, because even halfway up there was so much love and kindness. And Ānāpāna was breathing calmly—the air was so good and rich that he only needed to breathe very softly. But the two dogs enjoyed the peace and the view as well.

When they got to the top, it was utterly still. Nothing moved on top of Meditation Mountain, and Sam had reached his goal. But he also enjoyed the view—he could see forever, the whole universe spread out before him. Vi hadn't seen such amazing views before—the insights were all around her. But she also enjoyed the peace. And Mettā was incredibly happy, because in addition to peace and views, there was also the sheer joy and love of deep meditation. As for Ānāpāna, he had disappeared! They didn't know where he was. This is because the breath disappears on the top of Meditation Mountain.

That's how all these techniques work together. There's no difference between vipassanā, samatha, mettā, and ānāpānasati. There's only one type of meditation, and that's "letting go." The various names for meditation are just different ways of saying the same thing.

So let go however you want. The only meditation I don't teach is *ānā*-pain-*a-sati*—mindfulness along with pain. It was not taught by the Buddha. If it hurts, do something about it.

Could you provide some instructions on doing vipassanā meditation?

You don't *do* vipassanā; you just sit there, and the insight just comes by itself, like a meal served by a flight attendant. Or, to use another simile, you sit there under the mango tree and do nothing. You don't throw sticks up to make the fruit fall or shake the tree or climb it. You just sit underneath the tree and open your hand, and the mangoes, or insights, fall. That's how it works.

But you've got to be patient. You can't sit under the mango tree for a few days and expect results. That's nothing. Carry on, keeping your hand open and sitting still. If you move, even just slightly, that's when the mango will fall, and it'll miss your hand. Be very patient.

There are two types of patience: waiting in the future and waiting in the present. Waiting in the future isn't patience—it's waiting for something to happen, for the mango to fall; it's a state of expecting something, and it takes you out of the present moment. When you're practicing letting go, you're waiting in the present. Insights can happen only in the present moment.

During vipassanā retreats, the teachers normally suggest labeling or noting each action, thereby cultivating mindfulness. Do you recommend this?

No. Here's a story I invented to illustrate why not (with apologies for inadvertently offending any vipassanā teachers—it's meant in good fun).

One evening a rich woman was going to a talk at the local Buddhist temple. She told her security guard: "There are burglars around who know that I go to the temple, and they may try to break in. I have lots of expensive stuff, so please be mindful."

The guard said, "OK, madam, I've done many vipassanā retreats—I know how to be mindful."

"Very good," she replied, and off she went.

But when she returned home, she discovered that the robbers had torn through her house and stolen everything!

She was very upset and went to scold the guard: "I told you to be mindful! You learned about mindfulness at those retreats. Why did you allow me to be robbed?"

The guard said: "Madam, I was mindful. I saw the burglars going in and I noted, 'Burglars going in, burglars going in, burglars going in.' I saw them taking out all your expensive jewelry and I noted, 'Expensive jewelry going out, expensive jewelry going out, expensive jewelry going out.' I saw them drive their truck next to the house and I noted, 'Truck coming, truck coming.' I saw them taking your safe and putting it in the back of the truck, and I noted, 'Safe going in the back of the truck, safe going in the back of the truck.' I was very mindful; I noted everything, madam."

Of course, that's stupid; you're not supposed to just note. If you see burglars going in, you're supposed to do something, like call the police. Just noting is not enough. The same is true for meditation.

Learning unconditional love is the same as learning how to meditate—it's about opening the door of your heart. You practice by sitting, in the present moment, with all of its stupidity, its tiredness, its restlessness, and everything else that's going on in your mind, not wanting the moment to be any different from what it is. Loving-kindness and letting go are the same thing. As you learn how to meditate, your unconditional love grows and grows.

2.

Bear Awareness

Overcoming meditation obstacles with or without a furry friend.

Sometimes ridiculous thoughts will swirl through your mind when you meditate. You might catch yourself thinking about washing the shirt you've been wearing all day and then pondering whether to hang it on the line at the shoulder seams or upside down or whether to fold it in half. Being bombarded with reasonable thoughts seems bad enough, but, you might ask, how do ridiculous thoughts seep in?

The simple answer is that when you run out of reasonable thoughts, you move on to stupid thoughts. Any thought will do! It's just like watching TV when you're really bored: first you try to find an interesting program, but when you can't, you'll watch anything—even the most boring channel—to kill time. However, when you value stillness, you won't be bombarded by thoughts at all.

When you do experience some stillness, please don't be afraid of it. Many people are outside their comfort zone in silence. They're so used to thinking and they've become very good at it. They're familiar with thoughts; it's their usual hanging-out place. But no thoughts—that's weird! They're not quite sure what to do when there are no thoughts swirling around in their head. So they make some thoughts up, and it makes them feel good. It's comfortable; it's what they're used to.

It's just like when a man has been released from prison: he doesn't know how to relate to life outside. Inside prison he knew how the system worked and was comfortable. But leaving jail—that's weird.

In silence you're leaving the prison of thought. It's weird at first, but just relax into the silence. Don't be afraid, and you'll soon get used to it. You realize that you don't have to waste your time on stupid thoughts. After a while you learn to enjoy your house just as it is, and you don't want to waste time watching TV shows. Instead, you use your time wisely by being silent.

May the Peace Be with You

I can't sustain present-moment awareness. Thoughts always come between the breaths. Why? My meditation is always the same, even after three years!

Brilliant! Well done! All these people who try to gain something, they're just egotistical. They won't get anywhere that way. People always worry: "Oh, when will it happen? It's been three years and I still haven't got any results in my meditation." Whether it's three years, four years, ten years, or a hundred years, it's irrelevant—meditation doesn't work that way.

Have confidence. If you follow the instructions, it will work! Make peace, be kind, be gentle—that's all you need to do. When the mind is restless, make peace, be kind, be gentle. That's a goal you can always achieve. If you can't make the mind still or let go of the thoughts or get rid of the tiredness, you can always make peace with it. You can always be kind, you can always be gentle—that's within your power no matter what's happening. And that's all you need to do. Peace will follow along, and the joy of kindness and the beautiful equanimity of gentleness will be with you.

How can I stop the mind from planning into the future? Should I allow it to carry on? How do I bring it back to the present moment?

Just reflect that things rarely happen the way we think they will. The Buddha said, "Whatever you think it's going to be, it'll be something different" (MN 113). The future never turns out the way we expect. Because the future is totally unpredictable, it's a waste of time planning for it, setting all our hopes on it. We just don't know if or when something is going to happen. That's why I tell people that politicians shouldn't be elected on their promises—no one knows what the future will bring. And that's why I never blame politicians for breaking promises—they have to adapt to changing circumstances.

No one could predict the credit crunch, for instance, even the most highly paid economists. In trying to predict the future we're like these economists. It's a total waste of time to think about the future, and be so invested in it, when we have no way of knowing what's going to happen. If you aren't preoccupied with those kinds of thoughts outside your meditation, you won't be distracted by them when you're meditating.

You have mentioned that thoughts are invited, and all this time I've believed that thoughts just pop up by themselves! It scares me to think that I actually invite unpleasant thoughts. What triggers the thoughts to come? Is it that we crave certain feelings, certain emotions?

Exactly! Very good. That's what insight is. Because you're used to emotions, when they're not there, you feel a bit homesick: "I'm now happy and I miss my suffering." Here's a story about how this works:

Once upon a time there was a certain scallywag professor at Harvard who got kicked out for taking drugs and then went to India and became a guru. Sometime later, the father of one of his disciples went to the hospital with a painful disease. His daughter thought it would be a good idea to have her guru visit him. Her father, a conservative American, didn't want to have anything to do with such a hopeless, long-haired, good-for-nothing hobo. But his daughter decided to invite her guru anyway.

When her father saw this weirdo come into his hospital room, he said, "Get out of here—I don't want anything to do with you." The daughter went to his bed to talk to him. The guru, having nothing else to do, started to give the man a foot massage. After about two or three minutes of foot massage, all the man's pains disappeared. It was like a miracle. But then he shouted, "Get away from my feet!"

He preferred the pain to having to admit that this weird guy could do something doctors couldn't. He could have been free of pain, but he wasn't ready to have his mindset challenged.

It's amazing how attached we are to our philosophies, our religions, our views, and much more—so much so that we're willing to endure pain because of them. It's amazing just how attached we can be.

Sometimes you're attached to your pain because you're used to it. That's who you are. You become the victim of what happened to you earlier in life because you associate with it so strongly that you can't let it go. Letting go of your grief, your guilt, or your anger can feel like letting go of who you are and creating a totally different person.

If, however, you're able to let go of the image of who you think you are, you can also let go of all your associations with how you were hurt in the past or how you did rotten things to others. When you know that none of it is you, you no longer attach to it. You've got no sticky stuff—no sense of self—to attach you to the past. You don't identify with all that old stuff, and the old torturing thoughts about the past no longer come up. Why? Because it has nothing to do with you; it's none of your business. Isn't that wonderful? One of my favorite sayings is "None of my business."

As Good as It Gets

Much of the time I have sustained awareness of the breath, very few thoughts, and feel relatively peaceful. Occasionally a deeper letting go happens, and everything goes very bright and blissful. It seems that what stops the meditation from happening is a slight discontent, that things aren't as good as they sometimes get, combined with too much control. Why can't I let go of this control, even though I can see that this is what is creating the problems?

Just give it time. You can't expect every meditation to be a good one. Here's a story.

A man went to work on a Monday morning. In the evening he returned home without a paycheck to show for his work. He went to work again on Tuesday, worked really hard, but still didn't get paid. "It's a waste of time going to work," he told his wife. "I don't earn any money." But his wife told him to go, and so on Wednesday he went again, but again he wasn't paid.

On Thursday he went to work only because he had nothing better to do. Still no pay. He said, "What's the point of going to work if I never get paid?" But his wife ordered him to return to work, so Friday morning off he went.

On Friday afternoon his boss gave him a big paycheck. When he came home, he said to his wife: "Darling, I've finally figured it out. I'm only going to work on Fridays!"

You all know the meaning of that silly story: you get paid on Friday for all the work you did throughout the week. It's the same with meditation. Sometimes you don't get any peace or bliss, but then the next time you get the payoff. And you think: "Oh, why can't all my meditations be like this? Why can't all days be Fridays? Why can't they all be paydays?" It just doesn't work that way.

Remember, there's no such thing as a bad meditation—you're actually building up the spiritual quality of letting go and the wisdom of mindfulness and kindness. It may not result in bliss every time, but you're still making progress. You may not even see the progress, but it's there. And then you get the paycheck! Then you think there'll be a big payoff the next time you meditate as well. No way! Most likely you'll have to do more work. You got the paycheck only because of the hard work you did on all the previous occasions.

Understand that and you understand that letting go is something you build up. The paycheck comes only every now and again.

Trying not to control my mind, I practice mindfulness while walking or eating. I concentrate on the movements of my body, but unwholesome thoughts arise. As I watch, they subside. But as I let them go they keep coming like a train, thought after thought. Should I keep watching them, or should I let them go?

Let them go. And please don't use the word "concentrate"—it's like a swear word to me. The only "concentrate" a meditator should contemplate is concentrated apple or orange juice!

Meditation has nothing to do with concentration. And it's not a good translation of the word *samādhi*, which means "stillness." So please don't concentrate. That's using too much force. When thoughts come up, just let them go and you'll find stillness. Imagine picking up a glass of water and concentrating on holding the glass of water still. Look at it mindfully and try to hold it still. The glass of water will never be still no matter how hard you concentrate. You'll just get frustrated. How do you get the water to be still? Put it down. The water will become still all by itself. Let things go, and stillness happens. It's a mistake to concentrate in meditation.

Finding the right balance between letting go, so that the "glass" finds stillness, and focusing on your breath is for you to decide. If you focus on the breath and it gets unpleasant, you'll start thinking. If you're watching the breath and it's really nice, you won't think much. Don't watch the breath anywhere in particular. Don't watch it at the nose or at the tummy. Try to notice the breath without locating it anywhere in your body. Just know *that* the breath is going in or out but not *where* it's going in or out. That's the best way to practice. Just follow the direction of happiness. Don't work too hard.

When stillness develops, I feel peaceful and really enjoy the breath. But after a while my nose tenses up. Where should I notice the breath? Even if I try to notice it at the head or the chest, it's not comfortable. Sometimes I even hear heartbeats. Please advise.

The heartbeat is not comfortable to watch. If you hear it, just move your attention away and go back to the breath. Sometimes when you get very still, you may notice and become distracted by the beating of your heart. To overcome that distraction, a trick of focusing is helpful.

Imagine that I'm sitting before you and there are monks on either side of me. If you focus on my face, after a while the monk sitting on my right will disappear and you won't be able to see him anymore. That's just the nature of focusing.

Whatever is in the center of your "screen"—your field of attention—that's what your mind focuses on, and everything else is excluded. It's just like watching TV: after a while the mind fits into the TV, regardless of how big the TV actually is. You can't see the edges, just what's happening inside. Even if you had a triangular TV, it would look exactly the same as a rectangular one. That's how focusing works.

If you're watching your breath, you may still notice your heartbeat. But the heart is on the "left" or the "right" of your field of attention; your attention is not centered on the heartbeat. Just keep watching, centered on your breath. After a short while, you won't be aware of your heartbeat anymore; you'll be aware of only what's in the center. In the same way, if you're focusing on your heartbeat and your breath is on the edge, after a while you won't even know you're breathing. Whatever is the main focus of your attention will eventually dominate, and everything else will fall off your screen. This is the nature of paying attention. Don't have expectations, just pay attention.

Of course, just telling yourself not to have expectations doesn't always work. To get rid of expectations you have to program your mindfulness. Tell yourself: "I will not expect a nimitta. . . . I will not expect a nimitta. . . . I will not expect a nimitta."

At the beginning of the meditation, identify your main problem—excitement or sleepiness or whatever—and tell yourself: "I will not get excited. . . . I will not get excited. . . . I will not get excited when I get a nimitta." It works. You're programming your subconscious. When a nimitta comes up, that programming takes effect, and you won't get excited. Or, if you normally anticipate a particular phase of your meditation—"Here it comes!"—you can program yourself in this way: "When I get to that stage, I'll have no expectations. . . . When I get to that stage, I'll have no expectations. . . . When I get to that stage, I'll have no expectations." Say that to yourself three times and then forget about it. The expectations disappear. This is called programming your mindfulness.

If you haven't done this before, try a little exercise. In the evening when you go to bed, set your alarm clock to a few minutes after the time you intend to get up. If you want to get up at 7 a.m., set the alarm to 7:04 a.m. In this way you will have no fear in case the experiment fails. Then just before you go to sleep, say: "I will wake up at 7 a.m. . . . I will wake up at 7 a.m. . . . I will wake up at 7 a.m." You'll be amazed when you do wake up at 7 a.m., or one or two minutes on either side. It's incredible how well it works. How does your body know it's 7 a.m.? The subconscious mind knows it. That will give you confidence that you can program yourself.

Use the same method to program your mindfulness at the beginning of meditation: "I will have no expectations. . . . I will have no expectations. . . . I will have no expectations." Say it clearly, listen with as much attention as you can, and then it works.

I usually fall asleep when I listen to the rhythm of the breath. Several times I have almost fallen off a chair or a stool. Please help.

Isn't it weird how many people fall asleep when they're meditating but can't sleep when they go to bed at night? If you're one of those people, you can try reverse psychology. When you're meditating, try to fall asleep and perhaps you'll stay awake!

There are sleeping postures and there are meditation postures. Often your body will recognize this: "Yes, I'm following the rhythm of my breath, but this particular posture—sitting on my meditation cushion or sitting on a chair—is not the position in which I fall asleep." If you're sitting on your bed, however, you may be reminded of sleep, and therefore you go to sleep. It's not just *what* you do; your physical position and posture are also important. So make sure you have an appropriate posture.

If that doesn't help, try self-programming. Say to yourself: "I'm going to watch my breath, but please don't fall asleep. . . . I'm going to watch my breath, but please don't fall asleep. . . . I'm going to watch my breath, but please don't fall asleep." In other words, tell your mind that this is not sleep time: "Don't get confused. You're watching the breath to stay awake. You're not watching the breath to go to sleep."

You can also do walking meditation, because that will definitely keep you awake. I've never heard of anyone go bang into the wall because he fell asleep while walking. So do walking meditation and then breath meditation as a support.

Yet another thing you can do is to use a mantra along with the breath. But it has to be the right mantra. Don't breathe in "peace" and breathe out "let go," or breathe in "shut" and breathe out "up." You need something with more impact to keep you awake. As you breathe in, say to yourself, "I will die," and as you breathe out, say, "That's for sure." "I will die . . . that's for sure. . . . I will die . . . that's for sure." That mantra will usually keep you awake.

The Bear (and Other Furry) Facts

We used to have a nice teddy bear that sat right next to me when I led meditation retreats. Do you know what happened? Someone took it to auction it for the nuns' monastery! Now we're looking for another one. If you want to steal a teddy bear from your grandchild or something, feel free to donate it to the cause—joking!

But, seriously, the teddy bear was there because people are often too serious on retreats; they need some loving-kindness. If you are having a really hard time, you can sit with the teddy bear in your lap. You can get much deeper meditation when you have a teddy bear in your lap!

And a teddy bear can help when you're not meditating too. Buy one and put it in your office, so if, for example, you get overwhelmed by a fault-finding attitude, you can hug the bear and ask it whether there are any real faults to obsess over. It will remind you of gentleness, kindness. It doesn't have to be a stuffed animal—it could be a photo of your favorite monk, something that will remind you of kindness, letting go, and forgiveness. Hug your teddy bear or look at that picture and let the kindness flow back in.

Furry beings have other uses as well. If your meditations are filled with recollections of what you consider all the bad things you've done to others in the past, you need to do penance. The punishment is a hundred strokes of a cat. If you don't have a cat or a rabbit, borrow one. Hold it gently in your lap and stroke it a hundred times. If that doesn't work, then do another hundred strokes. The point of stroking a fluffy animal, especially a live one, is that you feel compassion and kindness. When you feel compassion and kindness toward a little fluffy animal, there's a good chance you can transfer that compassion and kindness to yourself. Then you can forgive and let go.

Get Still, not Stuck

In the last couple of days, I've seen a bright purplish light behind my left or right eye. It appears during the beautiful breath, which makes me suspect it's a nimitta. It doesn't last more than five or ten seconds, and as soon as I focus on it, it disappears. I read in your book that one cannot sustain a nimitta if one's mindfulness is too weak. Any tips on how to progress?

If you see a nimitta, don't try to focus on it! Don't try to make it last! Just make peace. Don't anticipate anything, don't expect anything, don't try to attain anything. As soon as you try to focus on it, it'll disappear. Don't do anything—just let it come to you. The best way to understand how nimittas work is to view them like the animals in Ajahn Chah's still forest pool simile. When Ajahn Chah wandered in the jungle, he would always try to find a lake or a river in midafternoon to bathe, wash his robes, and filter some water for drinking. After bathing and filling up his water jar, he would set up his mosquito net about ten to twenty yards away from the edge of the pool. He would then meditate there at night.

At dusk, he would sometimes keep his eyes open, because that's when the jungle animals would come out to drink and bathe. He had to keep very still because jungle animals are more afraid of humans than humans are of them. If they had realized that someone was there, they wouldn't have come out, no matter how thirsty they were. But if they felt safe, they would come out and play. It was great fun, like watching National Geographic Channel! But he would have to be perfectly still: if he moved at all or made any sound, the animals would run away.

That's how Ajahn Chah taught me about dealing with nimittas. If a nimitta comes up, you've got to be as still as Ajahn Chah by the forest pool. A nimitta is like an animal coming out of the jungle, and you've got to watch it the way you'd watch a timid animal. If you try to focus on it, it'll run away. If you get excited or afraid, it'll know you're watching and run away. You've got to be so still that it will not realize someone is watching.

It's a brilliant simile, because that's how it works. And it gives you something to imagine: you're like Ajahn Chah by the forest pool, and all these amazing things are coming out to play in your mind.

Ajahn Chah also said: "If you're extremely still, some really strange and weird animals come out to play, animals you've never heard of before. They are so shy that they only come out when you're perfectly still. Those are the jhanas."

If you move—"A *jhāna* is coming! Yes!"—they'll hear you, and they'll run away and won't come back for days.

So don't try to focus on the nimitta. Don't do anything. Imagine you're Ajahn Chah by a forest pool, absolutely still.

I'm stuck in the brightness. I can't move toward the nimitta. What can I do?

Don't move. The reason you feel stuck is that you're trying to move. If you just allow yourself to be frozen, wherever you are in the brightness, you'll have a good time, and the nimitta will come to you. If you try to get these things, they'll run away. That's how it works. It's like the story of the emu.

Years ago, an anagarika (an almost monk) at our monastery wanted to see an emu but could never find one. However, one day he was sitting very still in the forest for a long time when an emu came to him, lowered its head, and sniffed him all over. Just as with Ajahn Chah's jungle animals in the still forest pool simile, don't do anything, and they'll come out to play.

And what do you mean by "stuck" in the brightness? You're not stuck there; it's a lovely place to be. Enjoy it. Some people would be incredibly jealous. Just be content to be there. If you're happy to be where you are, you're letting go, and then the meditation develops by itself.

> A still mind is a mind that doesn't move, a mind that isn't agitated. It's not blank; you're always aware of something. Is the lake blank when there are no waves on the surface? It's still, not blank.

Be a Visitor

Can you explain how the ego affects meditation and how to manage it?

The ego is always controlling. The Buddha said: "When there is a me, there is a mine. Where there is a mine, there is a me" (MN 22). When you have a sense of ego, or self, you also have possessions, things over which you try to exert control. Your mind is one of those assumed possessions. For instance, on a retreat it may sometimes feel like you own your room, and as a consequence you want to control it and keep the sounds out. But it doesn't belong to you; you're only there for a short time. The point is that when there's a sense of self, there's also a sense of ownership and a desire to control.

Sometimes visitors come to Bodhinyana Monastery and say, "It's so beautiful, so peaceful, and so relaxing."

And I say: "Are you crazy? This is where I work. It's so busy. There's so much building and maintenance to do. There are so many telephone calls to make and so many questions to answer, and I've got to train the monks. What do you mean it's a tranquil place? This is a work camp!"

I realized that something was very wrong. I needed to find a way to rest and be the abbot at the same time. I decided that once a week, in the morning, I would imagine that I was a visitor, not an owner. Because I was a visitor, I didn't need to answer any questions—that was somebody else's job. I didn't need to do any building and maintenance work. I didn't need to do anything. As a visitor, I could enjoy the monastery. Only when you're an owner do you have responsibilities.

One morning a week, perhaps on the weekend, imagine that you're a visitor in your own home. Have some coffee, talk, and enjoy yourself. Let somebody else do the work. Just relax. If you're the owner, you have to be in control. If you're a visitor, you can let go and enjoy.

So be a visitor to your meditation cushion. Be a visitor to your body. Be a visitor to your mind. Then you can really let go, because it's not your problem anymore: "Mind, you can do whatever you want. You're not mine, and I don't control you anymore. If you want to sleep, fine by me; do whatever you want. Body, if you want to get sick, fine by me. I don't own you. I'm a visitor, not an owner." Or as the Buddha said: "Not mine, not me, not a self. It doesn't belong to me" (SN 22:59).

Whenever there's an ego, you want to control things. Be a visitor to this moment, not an owner. That's how you can let go in meditation.

I know that getting to stillness means getting yourself out of the way, but it seems almost impossible to let go of the sense of self. Although I want the sense of self to disappear, I feel I just keep encouraging it to stay. Please help.

Just stay in the present moment. This is a trick that allows you to disappear, because in the present moment much of "you" is gone.

Who are you? We define ourselves mostly by our past. You're a doctor, you're an engineer, you're a gravedigger. But that's just what you did in the past, not who you are *now*. If you let go of the past, really let it go, then who are you? It's very difficult to pin yourself down when there's no past. In fact, when you stop thinking and giving yourself labels, you start disappearing! All the things you take yourself to be—all those labels, all that past, who you've been told you are—let it all go. That's how we gradually let go of the sense of self.

We're also defined by all the things we want to be in the future, our goals and aspirations. "I'm an aspiring poet. I'm an aspiring meditator." Don't aspire to anything! If you aspire for things, you will just get the three "spirations": aspiration, followed by desperation, and finally expiration! Remember that all "spirations" have desperation in the middle. So have no aspirations.

If you have no plans for the future and you let go of the past, you disappear. When we trick you into being in the present moment, all those things that you define yourselves by just vanish. You're letting go.

Just follow the instructions: present-moment awareness, silence, watching your breath. After a while, you can ask, "Who am I?" And you find, "I'm gone!" Brilliant!

And if after meditation you feel like you've wasted your time, that means you're getting somewhere! Why were you trying to achieve something? Why did you think that time has to be used well and that you have to get something out of it at the end? Isn't life a waste of time? Soon enough you just die anyway, and after a couple of generations no one remembers you. What a waste of time! Life is a waste of time, except if you're doing something useful, like meditating.

> See if you can be a total failure today, that is, try to achieve absolutely nothing. Achieving nothing is an amazing thing to do: it's the great emptiness, when nothing is there. So let go, relax, have a wonderful day, and don't do anything.

3.

Waiting for a Painless Butt

The pitfalls of bad meditation kamma.

Just after tea one day while leading a retreat, I went over to our monastery to be with the monks. I wanted to have a shower and make sure everything was OK. One monk, who was going to teach at a prison, paid respects to me and left. But then he came back to see if he had left his bag.

He said to me, "I wasn't mindful."

I said, "No, no. You shouldn't look at it that way. You just weren't attached to your bag. Well done!"

You can look at anything from different perspectives. If you try to meditate and end up falling asleep, you can see yourself either as lazy or as compassionate—you must have needed the sleep, and you let your body have what it needed. If you're going to judge yourself, err on the side of kindness.

Most people these days are control freaks. We have been taught for a long time to exploit our body, forcing it to work hard. In Singapore somebody asked me: "Is it the case in Australia too that so many people get cancer? In Singapore the cancer wards are full." I think it's quite clear why so many people get cancer these days. It's because of the way we treat the body. We exploit it, we force it, and we don't give it enough rest. In the West, we think that laziness is bad, and we think that caring for our body is being indulgent.

Because we don't care for the body, many people get all kinds of sicknesses and die young. There was a Thai forest monk in Phuket, Thailand, who lived to be 117 years old and was pretty healthy as well. If you feel tired, go and rest. It will make you much healthier, and you will live longer. Relax the body and give it time to heal and release tension.

Look at how you live your day. You wake up using an alarm clock because you get up at an unnatural time for you. Then you rush around all day. Sometimes you don't go to bed until late. Because of that, you're tense. If you're mindful enough, you will feel the tension in your body.

When you're on retreat, you may need the first few days to unwind—use your mindfulness to know what your body feels like. Feel the effect on your body of those one or two days of relaxing, or sleeping if you wish. It's a wonderful effect. You feel the initial tiredness in the body and then the blockages being released. The whole body relaxes. And once the body relaxes, it's far easier for your mind to relax.

For the first two or three days, just indulge in resting the body. If you feel like sleeping, sleep, and don't set a time to get up. Allow yourself to wake up naturally. You can then have a cup of tea and a shower, and then go to meditate. You'll feel relaxed and your body will want to cooperate with you. Again, we were brought up always to force the body, always to control it. This is the opposite of working in harmony with things.

The whole of our Western civilization is about trying to control things rather than working with them. But on retreat you go back to a much more natural routine. By resting at the beginning of a retreat, you'll be able to do far more meditation toward the end.

Most people sleep more in the beginning, get back to their average in the middle, and sleep far less in the latter part of a retreat. Just do what's natural. The body doesn't need much sleep once it catches up on its deficit. So for the first two or three days, give your body the benefit of the doubt. If it says, "I want to sleep," let it sleep. In the middle of the retreat, ask yourself how much sleep you really need. For the last part of the retreat, say, "Ah, you don't actually need that sleep." However, if you're convinced that you're tired, then go to sleep regardless.

If the mind is separate from the body, shouldn't mindfulness overcome tiredness?

Your mind is connected to the body and influenced by the body. When the body is relaxed, the mind can meditate easily. The way you treat the body is also very important because your attitude toward your body is the same as your general attitude in life. It's this mental attitude that's important.

The attitude of forcing and controlling, of telling your body, "You're tired, but I don't care—you're going to meditate," is counterproductive in meditation. That degree of harshness—to regard everything in life as something to bend to your will—is what stops peace and stillness from happening.

In a sense the mind is both separate from the body and influenced by the body. The mental attitude that says "I need to rest now" is the same as the kindness that observes the process of meditation and says: "Let the mind be dull or restless. I will leave it alone. That's what it wants to do, and that's really all it can do." That degree of compassion, that degree of letting be, is actually the cause of stillness.

Sometimes I use the expression "meditation kamma." Just as kamma affects so many aspects of our lives, this particular type of kamma affects our meditation. Good meditation kamma leads to good meditation: peace, stillness, strong mindfulness. Bad meditation kamma leads to the opposite: frustration, boredom, tension, and struggle.

Good meditation kamma is making peace, being kind, being gentle, being patient. These are the three right intentions of the eightfold path, plus patience. This is good intention, good kamma. It cannot but lead to good results.

Bad meditation kamma is craving—I want, I want, I want—and ill will: "Mind, you're going to do what I tell you to do. I don't care. I hate sleepiness. I hate laziness." The reason I bring this up is that good meditation kamma is the seed and the cause for peace, stillness, and deep meditation. All you can really ever do is create the causes. Put all the conditions in place, and then wait for those conditions to ripen. You can't do more than that.

By making peace, being kind, being gentle, you're doing the maximum you possibly can to create deep meditation, stillness, insight, and enlightenment. This is your job. This attitude is the most important thing to encourage. If you have that attitude toward your body, you'll know whether you need to sleep or not. You're not being lazy—you're just making peace, being kind, being gentle.

That attitude will flow over into how you treat your mind. Again, it's not laziness if you're developing good meditation kamma. Sure, when you're asleep you don't get jhāna. But your attitude is creating the causes and conditions for jhāna in the future.

On the third, fourth, or fifth day of a retreat people often get frustrated and feel they're not getting anywhere. They've become so tense that they want to go home, and they feel they're wasting their time. I tell them, "Go to your room, lie down, and have a sleep."

"But that's being lazy!" they'll say.

"Go to your room, lie down, and have a sleep."

"But that's indulgent!"

"Go to your room, lie down, and have a sleep. Have a shower afterward and then a cup of tea."

Then, when they eventually do what I say, they come to the next interview and say: "Ajahn Brahm, it worked! It worked!"

Of course it works. I don't know how many times I've said that, and I've had a 100 percent success rate. You get some of your best meditations after you've relaxed. If you become frustrated and tense, it means you're trying too hard. So you need to learn to let go a little bit. The results are wonderful.

Good, Good, Good Vibrations

When I chanted *Namo Buddhāya* silently, as per your instruction, my scalp and hair had a tingling feeling, but it was a comfortable sensation.

That means you will become a nun! It's a sign. And the sensation is even more comfortable with a shaved head!

If you experience vibrations or some kind of energy flow during meditation, feel free to go with the flow. When I returned from teaching a retreat in South Korea, people were asking me, "Did you see 'Gangnam Style'?" I've never seen "Gangnam Style," but apparently it's dancing around all over the place. If that happens in your meditation, it must mean that you're doing Korean meditation!

Seriously, if you want to sway, sway. But when you do swaying meditation, please get off the chair, or you might fall off!

Sometimes, however, it may seem like you're swaying, but in fact you're perfectly still. Years and years ago a woman was convinced that she was swaying in her meditation. I told her that I was watching her and that she was perfectly still. I couldn't convince her, and so I said I would video her. Eventually she believed me.

You might think you're swaying, but you're not. It's just perception playing tricks on you. So if it happens, don't worry—just let it be and go with the flow. It will stop by itself after a while.

> If there is buzzing in your head, it comes from bees—and that means there must be being!

In moments of silence my mental chatter can get very loud. At times it's as if someone is talking to me, and it makes me feel like a schizophrenic, but I'm not.

If you were schizophrenic, you would say, "But *the voice* says that I am not." That means you can't be schizophrenic!

What's happening is that you're so used to talking that when you're not using your mouth, you're using your head. You're having a conversation with yourself because you have no one else to talk to. That's natural as you start out, but in order to overcome it, try substitution.

When I was a young monk and went to see some of the great forest teachers in Thailand for the first time, I was afraid. I was afraid that one of them would read my mind and tell others what I was thinking. I wasn't ready for my mind to be read. Remember, some of the monks and nuns may be able to read your mind, so be careful what you think. That should scare you into silencing your mental chatter!

No, good monks wouldn't read your mind even if they could. Just as you wouldn't read a trashy novel, we don't read minds.

Try substitution. Whether you use *Namo Buddhāya* or *Om maṇi padme hum*, whatever it is, do it with spaces in between. You then learn how to be silent. It's training to understand and recognize what silence is. The space . . . between . . . the words. Recognize it, become familiar with it, and then you become at ease with it, and it stays.

If substitution or noticing the spaces between the words doesn't work, you can use a mantra with the breath. In Thailand, they say "Buddho" with the breath. For Thai people that works. But for Westerners, or for people with an English-speaking upbringing, the best mantra I have found is, as you breathe in, you say to yourself, "Shut," and as you breath out, "up." "Shuuuuuut . . . up." After a while it sinks in and you do shut up inside. That's a good one. You learn how to be silent, and that's worth years and years of training.

If you learn how to notice the silence in life, you'll become very healthy, peaceful, and happy. When you watch carefully, you'll see many, many moments of silence throughout the day. When you value those moments, you can enter the silence. When you've trained in this way, you don't have to keep on talking and thinking, and you'll become a very wise and peaceful person. And a healthy one, too.

How do I progress from here?

You never *pro*-gress. You never go on anywhere. Stay where you are and go deeper into wherever you happen to be. There's no end to progress; there's only an end with *in*-gress: go *in*, never *on*. That's where you'll find the next stage.

Go on, and you'll always be restless. You've been going on all your life, always getting closer and closer to your coffin. Aren't you worried? Can't you see the coffin coming closer and closer? So don't go on, go in. Find out where you are. Go deeper into whatever experience you already have. That's the power of *in*-sight. You look within. If you look outside, that's called *ex*-sight—you get excited! So always go in and never progress. Stay where you are and go deeper into it.

I'm fully awake, fully aware, and my mind is still, not going anywhere. I keep sitting and my butt hurts. What am I waiting for?

You think you're fully awake, but you're not. You're only a fraction awake. You think you're fully aware, but you're not. You think your mind is still, but if it was you wouldn't ask, "What am I waiting for?"

Actually, you're waiting for a painless butt. Such a thing really exists! If it starts to hurt, get up and walk. Get some exercise. Sit on a chair. Some people say: "Nooooo, you've got to sit on the floor to get enlightened. Those people sitting on the chairs are losers; they're not really trying. They're namby-pamby cream puffs. Real meditators sit on the floor."

Your meditation can get just as deep whether you sit on a chair or on the floor.

Scary Stuff

I had a scary experience during a meditation session. My mind felt very heavy and dark, almost evil-like.

When you watch movies or TV, it's all evil stuff—vampires and monsters. Evil rocks! And that stuff can seep into your mind when you're meditating. But just remember that whatever you're experiencing, it's your attitude toward it that's most important. If you get scared of something, it may actually become dark, foreboding, and evil. If you just have an ordinary meditation experience, but you react badly to it, you create difficulty and darkness.

So change your reaction: "Ah, beautiful, empty darkness." Isn't the nighttime beautiful, when it's so dark that all you can see is the moon and the Milky Way? Darkness is great. And it's very heavy. Change your attitude and heaviness becomes good. I'm heavy, and that's good!

> Losing your mind is what you're supposed to do.

I had the feeling of spiraling out of control. It was very frightening. Is this normal, or is it time to apply the straitjacket? I hope you can shed some light on this darkness!

You're supposed to let go of control! The foreboding is what you added yourself. You're OK; it's just that you overreacted. I'll tell you one of my stories.

When I was meditating many years ago, I was getting into the nimitta stage, which is when you can see all sorts of stuff. My eyes were closed, but I had a very clear vision of a monster. I could see it right in front of me, with big bulging eyes, fangs dripping blood, and a necklace of skulls!

If that happened to you, what would you think? "Aaaaah, this is evil! I want to go home. A monster has come!" I knew the vision was a creation of my mind, and I realized that I could play around with it.

On the bulging eyes, which were almost coming out of their sockets, I put a pair of Ray-Bans. All I had to do was think it and it happened. It was really cool, like Elvis Presley with sunglasses. In its mouth, I put a cigarette. That's what I used to do at school—doodling on pictures and getting into trouble. I had good practice for my meditation! I then blacked out a few teeth, making the monster look as if it needed to see the dentist. On its head I put a straw hat with a flower in it.

The monster looked totally ridiculous—a joke of a monster! I laughed, totally humiliating it. It vanished, never to come back. That's the way to treat evil: just humiliate it.

Here's another story. A man who was visiting Bodhinyana Monastery told me: "I'm going crazy. I got some deep meditation, and then monsters came out of the paving bricks. Should I go to the doctor?"

I said: "No need to do that—just play with the monsters. Give them glasses and put hats on them—nice bowler hats if you like English monsters. Play with them."

I saw him later in the afternoon, and he said: "I've had a great day. It was so much fun playing with all those monsters. But they're gone now. Messing around with them took all the fear away, which was the real problem. The monsters weren't the problem."

So play with your fear. If it feels heavy, find out how heavy it can be. Imagine it's really heavy, like the fat Buddha.

The fat Buddha is supposed to be very auspicious. When I was in Korea, everyone looked at my round body, and I said, "See, I'm a bodhisattva!"

They said, "Very good, very good." They all thought it was very funny, because I'm supposed to be a Theravada monk, not a bodhisattva.

And one day, a Chinese lady couldn't help herself. She came up to me and rubbed my belly for good luck! I thought it was funny. I don't know if she got good luck, but she certainly gave it a go.

So that's what you do with heaviness. It's your attitude toward it that matters. Have fun with it, play with it, and then it's not scary anymore.

Got Light?

I have a close friend who tells me she receives messages from God. What she describes sounds like nimittas—bright lights and immense happiness. She says she sees formations in the clouds and that she dances with the angels. Does this mean that Christians can experience nimittas and jhāna, and that one day she can become enlightened too?

It could be. We need a bit more information to find out what's actually happening and whether it's really a nimitta, but it could be pretty close. And it depends on the messages she's receiving, because it could be a case of schizophrenia. You've got to be very careful in interpreting these things. If the messages make sense, then it's probably OK.

So if you ever have a nimitta and you hear voices, be careful. If you want to make money from the stock market, but you're superstitious and a voice keeps telling you: "Put money on this company, put money on this company," don't trust that. Here's a classic story.

There was a guy who normally didn't hear voices, but one day after meditation as he sat on his mat, he heard a voice whisper: "Go to the casino. Go to the casino."

He froze. This was weird.

Listening very carefully, he looked around the room. "What did you say?" he ventured.

"Go to the casino."

Wow! The voice was clear this time. And so he thought to himself: "Why not? Maybe someone is looking after me."

Arriving at the casino, he heard the voice again: "Go to the roulette table. Go to the roulette table."

He definitely wasn't imagining this. It was as clear as if someone were saying it aloud.

He went to the roulette table and the voice said: "Put ten dollars on number 17 . . . ten dollars on number 17."

That wasn't much to lose, so he got some chips for ten bucks and put them on 17. The croupier sent the ball rolling, and it stopped at . . .17.

"Yes! Yes!" he heard the voice saying, and then it said: "Put all the winnings on 22. Put all the winnings on 22."

Since they were all winnings, he put them all on 22. The croupier sent the ball rolling again, and of course it stopped at 22.

"Woo-hoo! Now put all the money on 16. Put all the money on 16."

The man now had about ten thousand dollars. That's some serious cash! Would he risk it? After all, if he walked away then he'd be a happy man. He paused to think about it for a moment, and then decided, "Ah, what the heck, I've come this far." With a final bet he put the whole lot on 16. If he won this throw, he'd be set for life.

By this time a large crowd had started to gather around the table, and the vibe was electric. The croupier sent the ball rolling once more, and as it spun a hush fell over the room.

Round and round the ball went, the only sound that of the ball rolling . . . until finally . . . edging closer to the slot . . . (This was a close one!) . . . it stopped . . . on 16.

A few punters screamed, breaking the silence, but the rest held each other tight, because they could see that the ball hadn't yet stopped. It teetered on the edge of the slot.

Time seemed to slow down as the ball balanced on the edge of the slot, the wheel still spinning. But then, the ball toppled a little more and bounced out, landing in the next slot. The crowd was stunned.

From the silence emerged the voice once more, now crystal clear: "Oh . . . shit."

Clearly, even celestial beings make mistakes. So if you hear a heavenly voice, don't follow it. It might give you the wrong advice.

Many years ago, after many days of focusing my mind in the present moment, I experienced a deep meditation on one of your retreats. This is what happened: I closed my eyes and focused on my breath. After a short time, all my senses shut off, with the hearing the last to go, and then the breath disappeared. Not knowing where to put my focus, I looked up and saw this massive, brilliant white light inviting me in. I let go to see what would happen, and I was pulled in with enormous power. Halfway in, I realized that to go all the way I had to let go of my sense of self, and I totally freaked out. With great willpower, I forced myself out. It was absolutely terrifying. I never want to go through that again. It felt as if my mind were being split between sanity and insanity. Now when you talk about nimittas and

jhānas, it still frightens me thirteen years later. On the other hand, it has led me to be curious as to what may have happened had I been able to let go. Can you elaborate?

Oh, you had such a wonderful chance! You wouldn't have gone insane, unless you think I'm insane.

That's exactly what happens: you see a beautiful light, you get pulled in, and it causes you to stop. It's the stopping that makes you fearful. But just go for it.

The fear is what stopped you from enjoying peace and bliss. You knew it was blissful, but you got scared at the last moment. Next time, please don't let that happen. If you see a beautiful light, merge with it, and you'll have the time of your life. The only bad thing that can happen is that you *don't* do it—that's the shame. If you have the opportunity again, please go in there. Anyone who has been in those deep meditations says how wonderful they are. They give great insight, great peace, great happiness, a great sense of freedom, and great health as well. So please, the next time it happens, go for it.

Thank you for guiding me to let go of my fears. After I achieved samādhi, it remained for a long time. When I left the sitting to walk, I couldn't see the carpet at all.

That was the fear of getting into deep meditation. Well, you've got nothing to fear and everything to gain. So when you start getting peaceful, just let go and enjoy it to the max. That's the whole point of meditation. Anyone who has had deep meditation says it's wonderful. Please join the community of deep meditators. Let go of fear and just have fun.

Today when I was meditating, I saw some yellow lights and later some unstable purple ones. I reminded myself to be kind and mindful and not to get excited. But I was able to hear clearly all the noise in the meditation hall. Is it normal to be able to hear when we see nimittas?

When the nimittas start coming up, you can still hear noise. But sometimes it's not a distraction—it's like hearing a noise some distance away. In other words, your five senses are closing down, but they haven't totally closed down yet. Sound is the last thing to disappear.

When the light comes, whether it's purple or yellow or polka dot, be with it. Relax, be kind, and just be aware. Then you'll be still and peaceful, and it will all be very nice.

While I was watching the lights, I kept reminding myself to be kind and mindful, but I didn't feel any happiness arise, which is what I expected.

Expectation is the opposite of *in*-spectation. Expectation is looking for something outside, something in the future, wanting something to happen. *In*-spectation, the opposite, is to look inside the moment. With *in*-spectation you don't have the problem of expectations, and happiness comes.

One afternoon, after traveling all around the world, tiring myself out, I had my first nice meditation for weeks. It was so blissful just to sit there, be absolutely still, and do nothing. Oh, what joy! So let go of your expectations and you'll be content.

When you want something more—whether it's happiness or lights—you can't enjoy what you already have. You've got lights? Wonderful! But you want more?! It's amazing how much people want. They get first jhāna, but no, it's not enough; they want second jhāna. They get second jhāna, but think, "No, I want the third, I want psychic powers, I want everything." And then they get nothing.

When you don't want anything, your mind becomes still. When you start wanting things again, you just create problems for yourself. However, don't learn the hard way; learn the easy way. In other words, make the mistake once, and don't do it again.

The Buddha tells a useful story about the training of four kinds of horses (AN 4:113). The first horse is really sharp. The trainer only has to get the whip out, and as soon as the horse sees its shadow, it follows the instructions and goes where it's supposed to. That's like a good student. I give the advice, and you listen to it and follow it straightaway.

The second horse is not so sharp. You have to tap it with the whip first of all—just to warn it without hurting it. The horse thinks, "I'd better do the right thing, otherwise I'm going to suffer." This is like the disciples who hear about other people's suffering and then think, "I don't want that." They let go, become content, and have a nice, peaceful time.

The third horse is a bit slow. You have to whack it, but only once. When you've been hurt once—you've been striving and getting frustrated and anxious—you learn from your mistake. You think: "From now on, I'm going to let go. I'm going to make peace, be kind, and be gentle. I'm not going to get into that again." Even though they're a little bit slow, disciples with this mindset are still pretty good disciples.

The fourth horse is really stupid. Whack, whack, whack, and it still doesn't understand. I always talk about the second noble truth—how wanting leads to suffering. Please learn how to let go—make peace, be kind, be gentle. Stop aspiring for things. Be here; don't try to get anywhere. How will you become peaceful when you're still holding the glass of water? You've got to put it down. Stop striving and use wisdom power, not willpower. Please learn, and don't be like that stupid last horse.

Make a mistake once or twice and then learn from it. Stop all this controlling. Just make peace, be kind, be gentle. Take it easy and be content. When you have that peace, you'll be grinning from ear to ear all day and night.

Once when I was staying at your monastery, I practiced mettā for a day or two, alternating with walking and a bit of letting-go meditation. The mettā grew and grew inside my heart, spreading through my body, and eventually there was an intense pink ball of mettā in the area of my heart. It felt so real, as if it were tactile. It was glowing and malleable, like soft, smooth, pink plasticine. Then it burst out of my heart, and my entire being was pink and mettā. It was the most exquisite feeling I've ever had. At lunch I wanted to smile at everyone with the most profound and deep love. But I was also in a vulnerable state: when I overheard someone being insensitive to somebody else, it hurt and shocked me deeply, and I fell out of mettā with a bit of an ugly thump. But it was still worth it.

That's what happens when you get into loving-kindness meditation—you get some nice nimittas and it makes you very happy. This is what you experience when you get peaceful and let go. You couldn't hold on to it because you were overdoing it a bit. But it's worth it just to have the experience of peace and love.

People who go through the light during a near-death experience (NDE) also say they experience more peace and love than they ever have before, just pure mettā. From such experiences, whether it's in meditation or during an NDE, you realize that pure love and pure ecstasy are one and the same thing. You can call it ecstasy, bliss upon bliss, or being merged in pure, absolute love.

The only way you can get there is by letting go of all wanting. Just keep on doing what I've been talking about. Make peace, be kind, be gentle; be as still as you can, and stop trying to control things.

Remember, there are two types of meditation. The first type is second-noble-truth meditation—"I want"—which leads to suffering. The second is third-noble-truth meditation—letting go of wanting, just being content and happy to be here, making peace with things—which leads to the bliss states. I keep on saying that people always make the same mistake: they always want.

WHERE IS YOUR MIND?

Once I've managed to sustain attention on the breath, is it OK to count the number of breaths to stop my mind from wandering?

If you've got sustained attention on the breath, the mind can't wander. That's the meaning of sustained.

If you're counting your breaths, this is the time to stop. If you've got full attention on the breath from the very beginning to the very end, and from the end to the beginning, the next thing is to create happiness. Once you get the breath to be happy—beautiful breath going in, beautiful breath going out—the mind doesn't wander.

Sometimes people say that they can't fix their mind on anything, that it's always thinking and wandering. But when they watch a football match they have full concentration for an hour and a half. Or they watch their favorite movie and can't take their eyes off it for a couple of hours, even if they need to go to the toilet. They just don't notice that they need to go while they're absorbed in the movie. It's only afterward that they think, "Oh, I need to go to the toilet." When you're watching a movie, you're focused. Why? Because you enjoy the movie.

Remember that it's the enjoyment—the happiness, the joy—that fixes the attention on the object, not force. When you start to enjoy the meditation and get to the beautiful breath, that's when you have the sustained attention, and the mind doesn't wander any more. Breathe in,

"Ah . . . this is so nice. . . ." Breathe out, "This is so nice. . . ." Don't forget the joy.

As long as you're aware of your breath, it doesn't matter what your body does.

I experience a long gap between the in-breath and the out-breath. What should the mind do at this time? I tend to start thinking.

Just be aware and be kind to the gap. Being kind to it means not trying to lengthen it to beat your record. If you try that you might die—you might asphyxiate yourself! So always remember to breathe in again after you breathe out. If you do that, you'll live a long life.

This problem may come from watching the breath rather than the stillness. When the breath stops, you don't know what to watch. Try to notice the stillness rather than the breath, and then you'll always have something to watch.

Do you understand what stillness is? Your mindfulness gives you feedback so that you can see whether the stillness is getting more solid and deep or whether you're getting more agitated. Watching the breath is just a way to move toward stillness. Stillness is more important than watching the breath. Stillness itself is the best thing to watch.

I have had some good meditations when there's just the breath and everything is quiet. Then I wonder, "Where's the mind?" I can't feel the mind. Is the silence the mind?

You silly person, you started thinking! Don't disturb the quiet. It's strange how people get very quiet in their meditation and then disturb it. Once when I was in Nepal, I walked up a hill and had an incredible view of the Himalayas when I got to the top. It was so beautiful that I wanted to take a picture. So I ran down to get my camera, but when I got back to the top the clouds had come in. I couldn't see the Himalayas anymore! Don't make the same mistake when you're peaceful. Don't disturb it; enjoy it! Don't start thinking, "Where's the mind?"

I was trained as a scientist. When I do an experiment, I don't try to figure out the result until all the data has been collected. If you try to reach a conclusion when you have only half the data, it may distort the result. So don't think about where the mind is or what's happening until the very end of the meditation. Then you can start thinking: "What was that? What happened?" In the middle of the meditation just be quiet and still, and allow yourself to collect more data. You shouldn't try to figure it all out in the middle of the journey. Wait until the end.

I've had so many moods passing through me today, from gratitude to sadness, from joy to fed-up-ness. Is there any benefit in reflecting on the impermanent nature of these states of mind in order to reach jhāna?

Yes, it's good to realize that you've got no control over your thoughts, over your emotions, over your moods. How often do you attempt to control? "I just want gratitude and no sadness." "I just want joy. I never want to be fed up." Can you control that? No, these things just come.

A student told me she was feeling grumpy. So I gave her a grumpiness license, a license to be grumpy at any time, for any reason whatsoever. Happiness is never a problem, but I gave her permission to be grumpy. How wonderful it is that you don't need to feel you're failing when you're grumpy. Exercise your right to be grumpy, whenever you want!

Do you feel guilty if you're grumpy? Grumpiness is part of life, so you might as well enjoy your grumpiness. In other words, it's out of your control. There are times when you're tired, there are times when you feel grumpy, and there are times when you feel really good. Which is the real you? None of them! So let nature do its thing. Then, when you're grumpy, you're happy to be grumpy, and that means you're not really all that grumpy. Reflect on this. All these things are impermanent. They're out of control. They've got nothing to do with you. When you understand this, you're free.

Another student confided that he was incredibly restless on the last day of a retreat, putting pressure on himself to strive for some peace till the very end. His mind was agitated; he couldn't stop thinking, wanting, striving. Finally, after sitting in the heat of his room all afternoon, feeling hot and bothered as he tried to meditate, he got up and went to sit on the bathroom floor. *Oh! How cool the floor felt!* And there, on the bathroom floor, he entered into the beautiful peace of meditation.

Isn't that marvelous?! Who knew that his real meditation room was the toilet—the place we let go of things?! You should never think: "Oh, there's only a couple of hours to go. I've got to work hard; I've been messing around." No, carry on messing around as long as you have to—there is no final push toward enlightenment. Striving will just make you hot, bothered, and frustrated. Just carry on doing what you do. I can't say it enough: Just make peace and enjoy every moment.

This is the beginning of my meditation journey, and my gift to you will be to continue practicing it in daily life. I love meditation.

That's great. When you like meditation—when you have a lot of fun, a lot of peace, a lot of kindness, a lot of happiness—my job is done. Then, wherever you go (even to the toilet!), wherever you are, you just love to meditate because it's so enjoyable.

In one sutta the Buddha says this is a path without groaning (MN 139). That's a lovely little saying. No groaning means a path of smiling and happiness, a practice that makes you happier and happier in this life.

> Meditation is not doing something, nor is it doing nothing; it's "nothing doing." "Doing nothing" is just another form of "doing something." Meditation is "nothing doing."

4.

Flying Buddha Air

Sit back, relax, and enjoy the view!

As far as meditation is concerned, *mindfulness* is the ability to know what's happening, to be aware. You can't be aware of everything, because there's too much stuff going on; so you put your awareness on the most important thing happening in the moment. Right now the most important thing is what you're reading, and so you're aware of the words on this page. There are many other things you're not aware of, such as the smells around you wherever you're sitting. As you develop your awareness, it gets stronger and stronger—you can literally "experience" more.

It's like the difference in a room when the lights are off and when they're on. When they're off, you might be able to discern shapes but not in great detail. When they're on, you can see things very clearly. It's the same with weak mindfulness versus strong mindfulness.

Part of the reason for going on retreat is to make mindfulness stronger and stronger, so you become more aware of what's going on, especially in your body and mind. With an increase in awareness, you go much deeper in meditation, and you understand much more of what's going on inside you. It's like turning up the lights inside.

When you strengthen your awareness, you can taste more of what's in the food, you can see more of what's on the ground, you can feel more, and most importantly, you can know much more.

There's also a significant connection between mindfulness and memory. When you pay attention to something with strong mindfulness, you can remember it very easily. The more powerful your attention is, the stronger the imprint on your mind. Or, as neuroscientists tell me, when you are very mindful of what's happening, more neurons fire. And when they fire together they wire together, as the saying goes. That is, when you're aware of something, it creates pathways in your brain, which is part of memory. In other words, every moment of awareness reinforces your ability to recall. That's why as you become aware, you remember much more of what you're supposed to be doing and where things are.

If you teach children to strengthen their mindfulness through meditation, they will get much better grades at school. They have to read a book only once or listen once, and it sticks in their brain. This is the result of paying full attention when the teacher says something. That awareness, that mindfulness, increases their ability to learn. It's really helpful for kids who have a hard time at school, any school, even university.

Nibbāna Unplugged

When the Buddha was on almsround, a man who asked him to teach some Dhamma almost immediately attained arahantship. If jhāna is necessary for arahantship, how was this possible?

That person was Bāhiya. In his previous life, Bāhiya had been one of seven monks under Buddha Kassapa (Ud I 10). These monks climbed a mountain, using a ladder to get to the top. Then they threw it away, making it impossible to get down. Meditate or die! One or two of them became arahants, and one became a nonreturner, an *anāgāmī*. Bāhiya was one of the remaining monks. When he died, he was reborn as a human being, as a sailor who was shipwrecked off the western coast of India. He lost all his clothes but managed to swim to shore, where he improvised a loincloth made of bark. People thought he was an ascetic holy man and started to bring him food and gifts. This arrangement seemed much more advantageous to him than working for a living.

Because people treated him like a saint, he began to think he was a saint. (This shows you why you've got to be very careful not to treat monks or nuns as if they're royalty or saints. If you do, they might think they deserve it, that they're entitled to being treated as special. That will destroy the Sangha.)

Then one of his old monk friends from his previous life, the anāgāmī, came down from the brahma world and said to him: "Look! You're not a saint. You've got a long way to go. You're just wearing these dirty robes, that's all."

Bāhiya then asked, "How can I become a saint?"

The anāgāmī said: "There's a Buddha around in the Ganges Valley. Go see him."

So Bāhiya went overnight to the Ganges Valley, which would have been impossible on foot. This indicates that Bāhiya had psychic powers. The very fact that he could hear his old friend, the anāgāmī deva, also suggests his powers. In other words, in his previous life, when he was on the top of that mountain meditating to death, he probably did attain jhāna.

When he saw the Buddha on almsround and asked him for a teaching, the Buddha said: "In the seen will be merely what is seen; in the heard merely what is heard; in the sensed merely what is sensed; in the cognized merely what is cognized" (Ud I 10).

Bāhiya understood and became enlightened. It was a very fast enlightenment, but it didn't happen just because of the words. Would you have become enlightened if you heard them? Bāhiya had a foundation in precepts, renunciation, and samādhi. That's why he became enlightened with a few powerful words of Dhamma. You need the jhānas and all these other things to become enlightened. Just one ingredient is not enough.

When the Buddha gave Dhamma talks, why did people get enlightened straightaway?

Number one, the Buddha was an incredibly powerful teacher. Number two, when you read about people becoming enlightened in a sutta, it wasn't just through the teaching in that particular sutta but also because of all the other stuff they did beforehand. Usually they had been meditating for years and years.

The *Theragāthā* and the *Therīgāthā* are the stories of the enlightened monks and nuns in verse form. They relate how they practiced for years and years to become enlightened. Venerable Anuruddha, one of the Buddha's chief disciples, worked hard for seventeen years before he became a stream-winner.

When you read these personal stories, you realize that the suttas just describe the final moments before their enlightenment. You see that these enlightened beings practiced for many years beforehand.

A classic story is about a nun at the time of the Buddha. She had been meditating for seven years as a *bhikkhunī* (female monastic). After seven years, she still hadn't had even a moment of peace in her meditation: no beautiful breath, no nimittas, no nothing! She couldn't meditate; she felt it was hopeless. If she couldn't meditate, she couldn't be a bhikkhunī. But she didn't want to go back to lay life, to the three crooked things: the broom she swept the house with, a symbol of housework; the ladle she made curries with, a symbol of cooking; and her husband (the third crooked thing)!

Because she wouldn't return to the three crooked things, there was only one choice. She got a length of rope, went into the forest, climbed a tree, and then tied one end of the rope to a branch and the other end around her neck! She was just about to jump when she had her first deep experience of bliss. She had let go.

Because she was about to die, she knew she'd have to let go of everything, including her body. At that moment she understood exactly what letting go was, and as a consequence she went into a deep state of meditation. That was the start of her enlightenment. But don't try her method. It's a bit too extreme.

Becoming enlightened is never easy. It takes time. Sometimes it's triggered by a specific event—whether it's trying to commit suicide or hearing a little story. Paṭācārā Bhikkhunī, meditating and getting nowhere, got insight when she saw the flame of her oil lamp go out. Simple little things may be enough to tip you over the edge and bring on your enlightenment. But it doesn't just happen all in one go. It takes a long time.

Why didn't the Buddha attain enlightenment while practicing jhāna under his two teachers?

The Buddha's two teachers before his enlightenment, Ālāra Kālāma and Uddaka Rāmaputta, got into states that were similar to the immaterial attainments, but not the real thing. This is so because the immaterial attainments are based on the four jhānas, but the Buddha never mentions attaining the four jhānas under those teachers (MN 26). In fact, when the Buddha reflected on the time he had got into jhāna before, it was when he meditated under the rose apple tree as a young boy (MN 36). This is a strong argument for the case that he did not attain jhāna under his first two teachers. If he had, he would have recalled that experience, which was more recent, instead of the one under the rose apple tree. So the Buddha did not attain the real thing under Ālāra Kālāma and Uddaka Rāmaputta because they hadn't experienced the real thing.

I read in one of Ajahn Chah's books that on the road to nibbāna, one minute the defilements dominate and the next the eightfold path. I've also heard that one must suppress the defilements so that they don't arise at all. Can you explain this seeming conflict?

Be careful when you read Ajahn Chah books. His words have been interpreted by translators, and the meaning may have been corrupted.

On the road to nibbāna, the defilements—greed, hatred, and delusion—have to be restrained. Ajahn Chah always said that. Yes, sometimes they come up, but you restrain them and use skillful means to let them go. You find ways of overcoming them. They'll come up again, but you weaken them and weaken them until eventually you overpower them. So there's no real contradiction, at least not in my memory of Ajahn Chah's teaching.

Can one choose not to enter into full enlightenment, or is it an automatic process? Is that what the bodhisattva does?

If you're a bodhisattva, you're not even a stream-winner. Once you're a stream-winner, once you're on Buddha Air, I'm sorry, but there's only one destination: nibbāna. You can't go to the pilot and say, "Please, let me out." It's too late! It's an automatic process, and you can't choose not to enter nibbāna or to postpone it. You've been brainwashed, and that's it.

Some monasteries teach that enlightenment can be gained only through vipassanā. Is this true? How do monks at your monastery split their time between jhāna, samādhi, vipassanā, mettā, and whatever?

That's so untrue. Please get the Pali canon out if you don't know this already, or ask the monks or the nuns. Every monk or nun who's done a bit of study knows that the only way to get enlightened is the eightfold path, nothing else.

This means that you can't become enlightened just by being mindful. You need to keep precepts, you need to have right view, and you also need samādhi, the eighth factor of the eightfold path, you need the jhānas. That's the only way you can become enlightened, according to the clearly stated teachings of the Buddha. He said it hundreds of times: The only way to get enlightened is the eightfold path, nothing else. This is basic Buddhism, taught for twenty-five centuries. It's a core teaching.

The reason the Buddha taught the eightfold path is that it's *the short cut*. He was wise. If there were a shorter path, he would have told us. If there were a way to avoid difficult undertakings like keeping precepts, he would have told us. If we didn't need the jhānas, which take a lot of time and skill to develop, he would have taught a sevenfold path. He was a compassionate being. He taught the eightfold path because we need all eight parts. Every part is important.

I always say there really are no short cuts. The problem is that short cuts are very attractive. Even when I check my email, there's always some spam, some get-rich-quick scheme. I don't know why people buy into that. The shortest short cut to becoming rich is to work hard! We don't want to hear that. We want a short cut. We don't want to work hard. But please—there's no short cut. There's the eightfold path, which includes jhāna, mettā, and vipassanā—the whole lot. Short cuts are just myths.

> The first factor of the eightfold path that's fulfilled is right view. That will lead you factor by factor to the end of the path, to samādhi, to jhāna. According to the suttas, each factor leads to the next, and as a result you see things as they truly are (MN 117). You get the wisdom and then the enlightenment. It's a sequential thing.

What's samādhi? In Ajahn Maha Boowa's book, he says he was stuck on a level of samādhi for five years. He said he was addicted to the peace and tranquility of that stage of samādhi. Please be kind enough to elaborate.

I don't know exactly what Ajahn Maha Boowa (a famous disciple of the Thai forest meditation master Ajahn Mun) said, because he didn't write any books. What you are referring to are translations, perhaps faulty, of his talks. But I know you don't get "stuck" in samādhi. You might get stuck with wrong samādhi, but you don't get stuck with real samādhi, the jhānas. You don't get stuck in the stages of letting go. Letting go means you're not stuck—you're free. The jhānas are stages of stillness, of letting go, of peace. How can you get stuck and let go at the same time? The jhānas really deserve to be called stages of letting go. The idea of this having anything to do with attachment is totally wrong.

If anyone wants to check out the teachings of the Buddha, go to the source—don't just believe Ajahn Brahm, Ajahn Chah, or Ajahn Maha Boowa. In the *Pāsādika Sutta* of the Dīgha Nikāya (DN 29), the Buddha says that anyone who indulges in the jhānas, who practices them again and again, can expect only one of four consequences: stream-winning, once-returning, nonreturning, or arahantship—that is, the four stages of enlightenment. This is what happens when you keep practicing jhāna again and again. You don't get stuck; you get released, you get enlightened. The Buddha said one should not be afraid of the jhānas, but that one should pursue them, make much of them, and cultivate them (MN 66).

So I don't know what Ajahn Maha Boowa actually said, but a state of samādhi should not be put down—it should be encouraged, as it is the path to enlightenment. People who say you can get enlightened without jhāna don't know what they're talking about. It can't happen. You need the jhānas; you need to be able to let go to attain enlightenment.

Remembrance of Things Past

If we let go of our past in meditation, why do we go back to our past lives after the jhānas?

All the past you remember is from this life, and that's boring. "I went to school, I had girlfriends, I got into trouble, I went to university"—that's not really interesting. If you wrote your biography, who would read it? So why keep remembering it? Let go of the past and be free.

Only when you've let go of the past and the future will you be able to spend long periods of time in the present moment. Your mind becomes very still and powerful, the body disappears, and you get to the jhānas. When you come out afterward you have power. You can ask about your past lives, and it's interesting.

First, you realize that you've existed before. Once you've had those experiences, you no longer have any doubt; you know rebirth is absolutely true. You should find this out before you die, because it changes your whole view of life. You won't worry so much about chasing money, pleasures, or power, because you know you've been there and done that. What's the big deal? Seeing the big picture makes you much wiser.

Also, you're not so scared of dying. You've done it before—*here we go again*—so this time you can get it right.

When other people die, even someone you really care for, it's not such a big loss. But if you believe there's only one life and a child of four or five dies, it's traumatic, it's terrible, it's unfair. When you know the child will be reborn again, you understand that the next time her life will probably be much longer. It's all fair in the long term. Understanding rebirth can have a hugely positive effect on people.

I wish our leaders understood rebirth. Whoever invades another country might get reborn there in his next life and suffer the consequences. Would you destroy a place if you knew you might get reborn there?

Our leaders are mostly old people, mostly old men. Perhaps they don't care because they think they'll soon be out of here; they don't take a long view. If prime ministers realized that they had to come back and live on this planet again, they'd take much better care of it.

Do you know why children cause problems and don't respect their parents? It's because they were grandparents in the past, and the parents didn't care for them. Now they're reborn and they're taking revenge!

If you knew that you were going to get reborn and that all these old people were going to get reborn, you'd invest much more resources in the aged. You'd realize that looking after old people is an investment in the future.

Understanding rebirth can change the whole dynamics of government. We pay attention to long-term benefits—such as the sustainability of our planet—because we're all going to come back here.

These are some of the reasons that it's important to understand rebirth.

How can you prove that there's life after death?

It's obvious—otherwise you wouldn't be here.

Who's going to get reborn?

You are.

Who decides if I get reborn?

You do.

Does every rebirth depend on the good and bad we do in this life? Who decides our rebirth?

You do. You decide where you get reborn. It's your fault you got reborn. Don't blame anyone.

How long can the mind or stream of consciousness stay between lives before it finds another birth?

What's the oldest ghost anyone has seen? In some old countries like England, people have seen ghosts that are 150 or perhaps 200 years old. But has anyone seen a caveman ghost, thousands of years old, say a Cro-Magnon ghost? That would be interesting, wouldn't it? Or a dinosaur ghost? It would be really cool to see a dinosaur ghost.

So maybe 150 years. And that's usually because people think they haven't died. You know what it's like sometimes when you're asleep—you're not quite sure whether you're sleeping or awake, whether your experience is real or not. You might have a dream of falling, and think, "I'm dying, I'm dying," and then you wake up and realize it wasn't real. At the time, however, it felt real. Being in the ghost realm is often like being in such a state of sleep—you're not really sure what's going on. That's why you can remain in that realm for a long time.

The job of a good monk or nun or anyone who is trying to help these people, is to tell them: "You're dead. This life is over. It's time to let go and take rebirth."

Did the Buddha ever say why we don't always remember our past lives?

I don't think so, but he did say how we should go about recalling them. And once you recall your past lives, you understand how *kamma* works.

One reason we don't remember our past lives is that the mind gets enmeshed with the brain of the present life. Sometimes young children can remember their previous lives. But when they reach a certain age their mind gets too enmeshed in their new brain. They're no longer able to access those early memories, except through meditation or sometimes hypnosis.

Do spirits exist? Are they good or bad? Can they harm human beings? You have said that after death consciousness gets separated from the body. What happens to this consciousness?

There are such things as spirits. I always have to tell people who ask such questions that there's one particular ghost that is very dangerous. I've seen it many times, and I've seen it possess people. When it possesses you, you don't speak your normal language, you can't do things in your normal way, and you can't even walk in a straight line. It's called the "bottle ghost." It lives in bottles of wine, beer, gin, whiskey, and vodka. When you open the bottle, it gets inside you, and if you're driving a car, it can kill you. That's why the bottle ghost is the most dangerous ghost in the whole world, and that's why we call whiskey "spirits." These are the really bad spirits. They certainly exist, and they're the ones people should be terrified of. But usually we're only terrified of spirits that don't exist.

THE BIGGEST LOSER

When an arahant dies, do the four aggregates that make up the mind follow the same pattern as the body aggregate—that is, break up and dissolve into some sort of nonphysical plane?

When an arahant passes away, all the five *khandhas* (aggregates)—body, feelings, perceptions, the will, and consciousness—stop. Nothing's left.

Where do they go? The Buddha explained to the wandering ascetic Vacchagotta that it's just like the flame of a candle (MN 72). When the flame is extinguished, where does it go? Does it go to the east? To the west? To the north? To the south? Or does the flame, if it's made good kamma, go to the heaven realm where all good flames go? Or does it get reborn in a pure land of flames? Or go to the ground of all flame being? Where does the flame go after it's extinguished?

It's a stupid question. The flame was just a result of the wick, the wax, and the heat. When any of those three causes is removed, there's no more flame. You're the same. When you pass away as an arahant, it's as if the flame has gone out. Peace at last. That's what the Buddha said.

"But I don't want to disappear," people say. "I've worked so hard to become enlightened. Can't I enjoy it afterward?"

No.

Remember, there's nothing there to begin with. Is there anyone there now? Who are you? You're not your body. You're not your feelings. You're not your perceptions. You're not your will. You're not even your consciousness. Since you can't find anyone at home right now, nothing is lost when the arahant dies, except suffering.

I've told many people that the practice of meditation and the eightfold path is about learning how to be a loser! Do you want to be a loser? I'm a loser.

I've lost all my money. I've lost all my family. I've lost all my possessions. I get rid of as much as possible. So being a Buddhist is being a loser. Being an enlightened Buddhist is being the biggest loser—you've lost all your attachments, and that means you're free. It's so nice to be a loser.

Is the knower the self?

No. The knower is not the self. The knower comes and goes. What is this knower, anyway? I'll give you just a taste of how this works.

When you close your eyes to meditate, what do you see? First of all you see the inside of your eyelids. If the light outside is bright, you see red, because the light goes through the blood vessels. You can still see a little, but it's uniform, dull, and dark. Because nothing is changing on the inside of your eyelids, after a while the sense of sight turns off. This is the nature of the sensory apparatus in your brain; it's wired only to notice change.

It's the same with hearing. If there's a constant sound of an air conditioner or traffic in the distance, after a while you won't hear it, because hearing too can only notice what changes. Smelling: as long as the smell around you is the same, you don't smell anything.

When you meditate you sit still. When you sit still and nothing is moving in your body, the brain turns off the sense of physical touch. You can only notice movement. Your body starts to disappear until only the breath remains. The breath remains because it is always moving. Then you calm the breath down, until it becomes so smooth that you hardly see any change from the in-breath to the out-breath. What happens then? The brain can only notice things that change, so even your breathing disappears.

Your five senses—seeing, hearing, smelling, tasting, and touch—have vanished. Wonderful! Those five types of consciousness are gone!

Then only the last consciousness—the mind or the knowing—remains. But as long as it's still, it too will start to disappear. Your knowing vanishes. Eventually there's nothing left. So what could be a self? That's called "the art of disappearing." When everything disappears, you realize there's no one inside. You're empty.

I've read that *anattā* means "nonself." Does that mean that whatever I experience is not mine, or that I don't have a self, or that things don't have selves or any abiding substance?

It means all that, but to understand nonself is a difficult thing. You won't get anywhere thinking about it; you'll just get confused. Instead of thinking about it, we experience it in meditation.

To give you a guiding principle, think of a stream of water, a river. You look at a river and it seems the same every day, but you know that the water you're looking at today is totally different from the water you saw yesterday. Now that's a good simile for the stream of consciousness.

What you take to be yourself may appear to stay the same, but if you examine it closely, you see that what you're looking at today is totally different from what you were looking at yesterday. There's nothing in there from yesterday that remains in there today. That's what we mean by nonself.

How can you recall past lives, but have no soul? Isn't the analogy of the candle being lit by another candle telling us that it's energy that leaves us to enter another life? And if the energy has a memory, why can't we call that a soul?

The Buddha used the simile of a stream of consciousness. What goes from one life to another is that stream of consciousness. A stream, or a river, looks the same from day to day, but the water you see today is totally different from the water you saw yesterday. The stream of consciousness is the same as a stream of water, a river: it changes from day to day, from minute to minute. The stream of consciousness hasn't got any essence, any core that's always there. It hasn't got anything today that was there yesterday.

If you get the idea of a stream, you understand why the Buddha didn't call it a soul, which by definition is stable and unchanging. The stream of consciousness is always in flux, always moving, just like a river. If you get that, you understand how rebirth happens: the stream of consciousness goes to a new body.

If there's no self, who's there to do the bad or the good kamma, and for whom?

As long as you think there's a self—I'm not talking theoretically, but deeply psychologically—you make kamma. If you can penetrate and see nonself as a truth and reality—not just playing around or thinking about it—really knowing there's no self, you're free from kamma.

This is why stream-winners are no longer subject to the lower realms, why they can no longer be reborn in hell, in the animal realm, or in the ghost realm. Why? Because if you know there's no self, then that bad kamma doesn't exist anymore—it's called *ahosi kamma*. If you realize there's no self, you can let go of all the bad kamma just like that. When you think you really exist, when that's your view, you also get all the baggage of the past. If you realize there's nobody home, letting go of the past is very easy.

So let it go. Stop sending yourself to the ghost realm or the animal realm. One person told me he wanted to be reborn as a dog, because then he wouldn't have to go to work. He could sleep all day, get good food, and just wag his tail and get stroked. He would just play all day and have no responsibilities.

Then I told him that during the first weeks of their life dogs get taken to the vet to get de-sexed! When I told him that, he didn't want to be a dog anymore. He hadn't thought it through properly. So be careful about where you decide to send yourself.

You have said that "doing" reinforces the ego. How did the Buddha strive to build up a Sangha and teach without reinforcing the self? How do we do it at work? Is it by being mindful, by acting from anattā? Thanks. You rock.

Actually, I am like a rock—like the size of a large rock! Doing does reinforce the sense of self. But there are some actions, such as those based on compassion and kindness, that are different. These actions have nothing to do with you—they're about helping and serving others.

Then there's meditation, when you don't do anything at all. But you can't continue like that when you go back to work. Otherwise you'll be crossing busy streets in the city while noticing, "Lifting my foot . . . moving it forward . . . setting it down. . . ." There's a story about this.

A vipassanā practitioner did a slow-walking vipassanā retreat. On Monday morning, after he had finished the retreat, he went to work at Perth Zoo. As . . . he . . . went . . . in . . . to . . . work . . . he . . . was . . . so . . . mind . . . ful . . . that . . . he . . . walked . . . ve . . . ry . . . slow . . . ly . . . and . . . talked . . . ve . . . ry . . . slow . . . ly . . . mind . . . ful . . . of . . . ev . . . e . . . ry . . .word. . . .

The head zookeeper was wondering what work he could give a guy who was so incredibly slow. Being smart, he said, "You can look after the tortoise enclosure."

"O . . . K. . . . I . . . will . . . look . . . af . . . ter . . . the . . . tor . . . toi . . . ses . . . ," he said.

Off he went, mindfully walking to the tortoise enclosure. At lunchtime the zookeeper thought to check up on the guy to make sure he was OK. When he got to the tortoise area, the gate was open and all the tortoises were gone.

The zookeeper asked, "What happened?"

The meditator replied, "Well . . . I . . . just . . . op . . . ened . . . the . . . gate . . . and . . . whoo . . . oo . . . oosh!"

That's a stupid joke, but I love it, because that's what happens when you walk very slowly in meditation. Compared to you even tortoises go whoosh! So when you're working, please work at a reasonable pace. When you're crossing the road and driving the car, please get back into gear.

So, yes, you do and strive when you're out there working, just as the Buddha did when he was building up the Sangha. But when the Buddha wanted to stop, he stopped and did nothing.

Is there any practice for reducing the ego that one can do when not meditating?

You can do something stupid and ridiculous, like the kangaroo walking meditation (see page 10). That will really lessen your ego! Try it. Straightaway it brings you happiness, and it makes other people laugh too. You're being compassionate. That's one way of reducing the ego.

Another way of reducing the ego is to stop controlling. When you control, you build up the force of the ego. The more you control, the bigger the ego. The more you demand, the bigger your sense of self. The more you let go and flow with things, the more you disappear. When you let go, when you're kind, when you forgive, your ego gets smaller and smaller. Stop controlling and your ego disappears.

> Take the "H" from Hinayana, the "aha" from Mahayana, and the "yana" from Vajrayana. What do you get? The Hahayana—which is my tradition. Put all those traditions together and make it a fun path. A lot of those traditions were not taught by the Buddha. The Buddha taught the four noble truths and the eightfold path. The simpler it is, the more likely it is to be straight from the Buddha.

Kamma Suttas

How do you explain good people getting negative consequences but bad people getting positive results? Is this the law of cause and effect, the law of kamma, in the true sense?

No, it doesn't happen that way. Do you really know those "good" people? Sometimes someone appears to be good on the surface, but you don't really know what they're up to. If they get negative consequences, it's because they haven't actually been all that good.

And people who do evil don't get positive results. Many of the people you think are doing well in life—wealthy or famous people—actually have terrible lives. Some of them are on hard drugs. Look at what happened to Michael Jackson. It seems that he was taking lots of drugs just to sleep at night. He was very wealthy and famous, but he had a terrible life. Positive results cannot always be measured in money and wealth.

There are people who aren't very rich but who are happy. They may not be terribly successful, but they have a nice and peaceful life. The really positive results in life, the results of real good kamma, are things like contentment and happiness. Often the simple life is the best life. People with lots of expensive possessions are often owned by their possessions. They're not free at all.

People who *really* do good get good results, but sometimes it can be very hard to see. Look at how happy and content they are. That's the best indication of whether they're truly good people.

I truly believe that negativity attracts negative things in life. What I don't understand is why the wise Ajahn Chah had to suffer physically with his illness at the end of his life or why the Buddha's disciple Mahāmoggallāna had to die by being bashed to death.

Sometimes the kamma from the past is so strong that you have to experience the results, and there's nothing you can do about it. What you can do, however, is have the right attitude: just let it be—make peace, be kind, and be gentle with whatever you're experiencing. It doesn't matter what the object of your mind is—whether you suffer or you're free depends on your attitude. Are you trying to get rid of things? Are you upset? Are you frustrated and trying to get somewhere else? Or are you at peace? Even with pain, really strong pain, if you let it be, accept it, open the door of your heart to it, and welcome it, it just vanishes. I've experienced this myself, and so have others.

The Buddha said there are two parts to pain: the physical and the mental. The physical pain is tiny compared to the mental anguish. If you let go of the mental anguish, the physical pain is easy to endure. People can endure physical torture, but the mental stuff can hurt so much that you may wish you were never born.

In the suttas, is it bad kamma to doubt the Buddha?

It's not bad kamma to doubt the Buddha if it's real doubt. It's not a problem—that's just being honest. But if you want to harm the Buddha or you curse him, that's bad. And stopping others from seeing the Buddha is also very bad. So you don't really make bad kamma by doubting. And doubt is good in the sense that it makes you ask questions.

In your book *Mindfulness, Bliss, and Beyond,* you mention that if your nimitta is dirty or dull, you may need to clean up your act.

Yes, exactly. Remember that the nimitta you see in meditation is a reflection of your mind, the inner part of you. When the nimitta appears, you're seeing your own mind. The brilliance of the nimitta reflects the brilliance of your mind. At this stage you cannot fake anything; you're seeing your mind directly.

If you bang the doors, always complain about everyone else, never clean up anything, and always ask stupid questions, your nimitta will look dirty, smeared, and shabby. It'll be like a mirror that needs cleaning because it's covered with fingerprints and dust.

On the other hand, when very pure hearted and kind people get a nimitta, it's really gorgeous. These are the people who're always willing to help others. They'll open the door for you, and if you're a bit sick, they'll offer you a cup of tea or even breakfast in bed. You just know they're beautiful people.

So the nimitta reflects the purity and goodness of your heart, and yes, your accumulated kamma matters. If you've been a very generous person, kept your precepts, helped people who are more needy than you—if you've always been kind and generous—your nimitta will be brilliant.

Can somebody's bad kamma from the past influence another person to do bad kamma now? For instance, did Venerable Mahāmoggallāna's bad kamma from the past influence the criminals who killed him to do bad kamma?

According to legend, Mahāmoggallāna, one of the Buddha's chief disciples, had murdered his parents in a previous life, and so in this life he had to endure being beaten to death. Did the thieves *have* to do that to ensure the ripening of Mahāmoggallāna's kamma, or were the two things independent? They were independent. The thieves did their kamma, and would eventually have to pay the price, whereas Mahāmoggallāna wore off the really bad kamma of killing his parents.

Everyone's kamma is his or her own. We are the owners of our kamma: my kamma is mine and yours is yours. But we can influence one another. I had the good kamma of being able to stay with Ajahn Chah, and now that good kamma is affecting my students. This in turn influences my students' kamma in a positive way. Isn't that wonderful? We do influence one another, but we all own our own kamma.

Can you please explain the relationship between eating meat and kamma? I don't kill animals, but I eat meat. Am I responsible for the killing? I like the taste of meat, and eating meat is part of our culture.

If you can be vegetarian, fine, but don't judge people who are not. Just do the best you can.

I was vegetarian before I was ordained. Once I became a monk, I had to eat whatever I was given, which was often meat. I'm sure you've heard the stories of eating frogs and snails! I would've given anything to have some vegetarian food in my early days as a monk.

Once, while I was still a layman, my girlfriend cooked me dinner. She forgot I was vegetarian and made a meal with meat. I refused to eat it. Imagine someone going to all the trouble of preparing a delicious meal for you, and then you refuse to eat it because of the meat! That was the end of that relationship.

Later, I realized that it had been a stupid thing to do. I was the one who was wrong. It was as if I loved animals but hated people. I was cruel to her, and I'm not proud of it. I admit I made a mistake. I could have just eaten the meal and said kindly: "Thank you. Next time, please make it vegetarian." That would have been an appropriate thing to do, instead of acting like a vegetarian terrorist. So, if you can be vegetarian, fine, but please don't be a terrorist.

Samsara sucks! However, escape is possible through the eightfold path. Doesn't this indicate that the universe is fundamentally benevolent and a force for good? Otherwise no escape would be possible.

That's one way of looking at it. But it's not really that the universe is benevolent; the universe just *is*. Samsara can be troublesome, but if you know how to work the system, how to make good kamma, the universe isn't so bad.

If you really want to get out of the universe, out of samsara, the way out is the path of bliss upon bliss upon bliss. Some years ago I used the simile of a meteor in the sky, a shooting star. Meteors are usually lumps of ice that whirl around the solar system for millions of years and then suddenly meet the atmosphere. That's when you see them as beautiful streaks of light as they finally come to their end. The meteors have been around for such a long time, but now you see their beautiful, brilliant ending.

Human beings are just the same. They go round and round samsara, hundreds of thousands of times. Then they meet the Dhamma, and they're like a meteor meeting the atmosphere of the earth. They become brilliant—a shining shooting star, lighting up the night sky, gorgeous, a wonderful flash, and then . . . they're gone.

> At the time of the Buddha, there were a lot of wanderers, including Jains, who were female—people of both genders practiced religion then. But the Buddha did start the female Sangha. So he was one of the first feminists, a fighter for equality, of which I thoroughly approve.

Why are Buddhist nuns often overlooked when it comes to supporting the monastics? Is there anything else we can do to help raise money for the nuns' monastery?

At one fundraiser I told a story about Ajahn Chah. It's a great story.

There was a man from Sydney who had heard of Ajahn Chah and wanted to speak with him personally. He flew to Bangkok, got a train to the district of Warin Chamrap, almost four hundred miles from the capital, then took a taxi from there to Ajahn Chah's temple. It was a real expedition to get to the monastery.

He found Ajahn Chah where he always was during the day: under his hut, receiving guests from around the country and a few foreigners as well. They asked all sorts of questions, usually about their marriage or business, because Ajahn Chah was famous for being wise. People really waste your time when you're wise. Instead of asking about meditation, they ask about all sorts of stupid stuff.

However, because Ajahn Chah was kind, he answered everyone's questions. The guy from Sydney had something important to ask, but couldn't get close to Ajahn Chah because of the large crowd surrounding him. After waiting several hours, he figured that his long journey was in vain, so he decided to leave. As he was leaving, he noticed some of the monks sweeping. He thought, "To make my trip worthwhile, at least I can do some good kamma by helping to sweep." This was an important point: He was doing good kamma, not just thinking of himself.

As he was sweeping, he felt a hand on his shoulder. He turned around, and found that the hand belonged to Ajahn Chah. Ajahn Chah was going to another appointment, but he realized that this Westerner had come all the way to see him, so he stopped for a minute to give him a short teaching. Later, the Australian told me what a powerful teaching it had been, even though it was so short. Ajahn Chah told him, "If you're going to sweep, give it everything you've got."

He knew that the teaching wasn't just about sweeping. If you're working, give it everything you've got. If you're meditating, sit down, let go, be still, and give it everything you've got. If you're resting, if you're lying down in bed at night, give resting everything you've got.

So, at the fundraiser, I told the donors that if you are giving a donation, give it everything you've got! Nice try, but it didn't work.

But to answer your question: Please keep in mind that the bhikkhunīs at Dhammasara are quite historic within the Theravada tradition. We've got heaps of monasteries for monks in Perth, but monasteries for nuns are very rare. I try to get people everywhere to keep monasteries simple. But some of the monasteries are as elaborate as palaces. What a waste of money! We've got a long waiting list of women wanting to become bhikkhunīs at our monastery, but there's no housing for them.

If you want to make a donation, please do so to the nuns' monastery. When you think about what you've done in your life, you'll see that this was really worthwhile. You gave to something historic, something that's going to make a big difference.

When I was still a layman, I heard a talk by a Tibetan nun about an orphanage she was running in Kalimpong, in northern India. I was so inspired that the next day I got ten pounds out of my bank account to give her a donation. That was two or three weeks' worth of food money, which meant I was hungry for that period. Although I didn't starve, I didn't have as much to eat as I normally would, and that hurt. However, that was one of the best donations I've ever given. I've never forgotten it because it wasn't easy. When you make a donation that hurts or that makes a serious dent in your bank balance, that's really good kamma.

So please make donations to the nuns' monastery, and I guarantee that you will never regret it. When you die, you will think: "What have I done in my life? What service have I given?" You will then remember that you helped build a monastery for nuns, something very rare. I'm really disappointed that people don't support the nuns more.

If a person insults or verbally abuses the Buddha and the Dhamma, or has a misunderstanding, should we explain things to them and correct them? Would we be creating bad kamma if we kept quiet?

No one can abuse the Buddha or the Dhamma; they can only abuse themselves. When people say bad things, they're only destroying their own credibility. The Buddha is beyond denigration. They can blow up a Buddha statue, they can shout, they can abuse, they can make mocking cartoons about the Buddha, but does that really affect the Buddha? Of course not. It can affect people, though. It's easy to forget about the Buddha's teachings and sometimes even kill those who desecrate the Buddha. But there's nothing Buddhist in that.

Let me share a story from Guantanamo Bay that illustrates this point. Some marines at Guantanamo Bay were accused of flushing a copy of the Koran down the toilet, and Muslims around the world were up in arms about the desecration of the Islamic holy book. Someone from an Australian newspaper phoned me up. He was writing an article. He had already contacted the leaders of all the other major religions in Australia and asked them the same question. Now he was calling me as one of the leaders of Buddhism. The question was, "If someone took a Buddhist holy book and flushed it down a toilet, what would you do?"

"I'd call a plumber!" I said, which made the journalist laugh.

He said: "That's the first sensible answer I've had all day. Can I publish that, please?"

You can flush as many Buddhist books down the toilet as you like. You can blow up the statues. You can burn down the temples. You can machine-gun the nuns and the monks. But I would never allow you to flush Buddhism down the toilet. I would never allow you to destroy forgiveness, peace, and kindness.

The buildings, the statues, the books, even people's bodies—these are called containers. The content is what's really important. What does the Buddha signify? What's written in the books? What do the monks and the nuns teach? Don't let that get flushed down the toilet.

So it doesn't really matter if someone abuses the Buddha. I'll forgive him. I'll be kind to him. That way he'll never destroy Buddhism.

Do Buddhists have confession? Do monks give forgiveness for sins, as the Catholic Church does?

Do we give confession? Yes. If you want to confess all your sins to me, then please do so. I can then use that for blackmail to raise funds for the nuns' monastery! Once I know what you've really been up to, I can contact your wife, but only if you don't give a big donation!

No, we don't do confession, but you can confess to yourself. You know what you've done, so forgive yourself and let it go. A priest or a monk cannot really forgive you anyway. The only person who can truly forgive you is yourself.

You can ask forgiveness from someone you've hurt, and she might say: "Oh, forget it. Never mind, we all make mistakes." She'll forgive you, but does that stop you from feeling guilty? You may still feel guilty, because the only person who can really forgive you is yourself.

Sādhu means "it's good," "it's cool." It means "awesome," "well done," "cheers," "good on you." It's a word of appreciation.

5.

Everyday Kindfulness

The prescription for all that ails you.

A few years ago at a retreat in Sydney, there was a man who made loud breathing noises during meditation. A couple of days into the retreat I received several notes in the question box complaining about this and asking me to tell people to breathe quietly. That man was dying of nose cancer. The doctors had given up on him, and this was his last throw of the dice, as they say—to see if meditation could keep him alive. As soon as I told people this, there were no more complaints, just a lot of compassion: what a wonderful thing it was that he was giving meditation a try. He was making the noise because he had a big tumor in his nose.

On the last day of the retreat, he wanted an emergency interview. He told me that during the previous couple of hours an amazing thing had happened: He was meditating in the usual way, breathing through his mouth, when he heard a "pop"—he could breathe through his nose! It lasted only about a minute before the tumor closed the passageway again. I thought that he'd left it too late, that had he started meditating earlier he might have got the cancer into remission. Anyway, he just carried on meditating.

A few years later, a man came up to me in Sydney and said, "Do you remember me?" He was that man. He said he had carried on meditating, the tumor had shrunk away completely—full remission—and now he was spending the rest of his life teaching meditation to others.

The other great story is from a retreat I gave at our previous meditation venue in north Perth. A guy came to the retreat wearing a rubber face mask. He told me at the beginning that he wasn't sure if he would last the full nine days because he had a very severe case of psoriasis. The rash was all over his body (he lifted up his trousers and pulled up his shirt to show me), and it itched like hell. He wore the face mask so he wouldn't scratch the skin off his face. He was in a state of constant torment.

He managed to stay the whole nine days, which really impressed me. When he came to see me at the end, he wasn't wearing the face mask. He lifted up his shirt and pulled up his trousers. The rash had completely disappeared except for a small band around his ankles, one or two inches wide. It was wonderful to see the relief on his face. He was free from the constant torture.

So, yes, meditation does work. You just have to relax, let go, be still, and stop trying to control things. If you meditate to get rid of the illness, it won't happen. If you meditate just to make peace, be still, and be kind, then it goes. That's why many doctors recommend meditation to their patients.

WHISPERED WORDS OF WISDOM

How can we use what we've learned in meditation to cure illness? Or should we be so content that we don't try to recover and just let it be?

Just let it be, and you'll recover. If you try to get better, you'll get worse. A lot of sickness is due to stress, working too hard, tiring yourself out. If you want to overcome sickness, you first have to accept it, to stop fighting it. If you just relax and let it be, it usually doesn't last very long. If you fight, you create stress, and then the illness gets worse. Just follow the meditation instructions you've been given and you'll get better.

I know we should accept the past and let it go, but sometimes I'm reminded of very unpleasant events that traumatized me. How do I learn to accept the past in meditation? How do I know I have succeeded in letting go of the past?

You'll know you've succeeded when it doesn't bug you anymore. In other words, you'll feel that it's just something that happened in the past: "Big deal. I've let it go. It's not important anymore."

The reason it keeps bugging you is that you give it importance. Somehow or other you think that you should really deal with it, that you aren't allowed to let it go, and that you have to keep punishing yourself over and over again. Sometimes that's a tendency in Western culture, but it affects the East as well. You really think you deserve punishment, blame, and suffering because of something you've done.

Some people even think they should suffer although they haven't done anything wrong. They just think they deserve to suffer! That's absolutely crazy as far as Buddhism is concerned. In Buddhism, even if you've done something wrong, there's no punishment.

Just acknowledge that you've made a mistake, that you've done something stupid. Everyone makes mistakes. Then forgive yourself and learn from it so you don't make the same mistake again. That's all we do: acknowledge, forgive, and learn. No punishment.

When there's no punishment, it's much easier to let go. When you think there's punishment involved, it complicates things. We tend to hide the truth and not admit what we've done. We don't want to deal with it because we think it's going to hurt. We can't let go because we're avoiding the punishment, which we think we deserve.

So please understand that there's no punishment, and then it'll be very easy to let go of the past. Don't take it on and hurt yourself. You don't deserve that. In fact, when you do something wrong, you should tell everybody about it to give them a laugh.

When you get frustrated with your disciples' actions and behavior, do you feel like quitting your job as a spiritual teacher and letting them go?

You never get frustrated; you just think it's all good fun. When people do something really stupid, you think: "Wow! That's really funny."

Number one, you expect people to do stupid things. Number two, when they do stupid things, you always see the humor in it—you see how silly people can be. You can then tell everyone about it, and that makes them laugh.

We all do stupid things at times, so there's no reason to get frustrated.

Frustration is a sign that you're trying to control, trying to achieve this and get that. I tell others not to be control freaks, and that's also how I act. I'm not a control-freak abbot. I don't even control my own mind—I let it be, and then it's much more peaceful, still, and happy. So by not controlling the monks, I don't get frustrated when they do stupid things.

I did hear that one of the anagarikas (trainees) had gone on strike! Instead of getting frustrated, I thought: "It's really funny. I don't know what he's going to do. He can go on strike as long as he likes—as long as he doesn't start a union and get all of the other anagarikas to go on strike as well. If he joins up with the unions in Perth, I'll be in trouble! But other than that, it's just funny."

So laugh, and don't take it seriously. Frustration is a sign of stupidity, a sign of too many expectations. Lower your expectations. Have no expectations at all, especially in your meditation, and you won't get frustrated.

What's the difference between discipline and control? Where do you draw the line between observing strict discipline and being a control freak?

I've had this question many times before. The answer I give is taken from *The Art of War*, in which a Chinese general describes how he maintained the best discipline in the imperial army.

The emperor summoned the general and asked: "What's the secret behind your discipline? Your soldiers always follow your orders and never rebel. Why? What's the secret?"

And the general said, "My soldiers always follow my orders because I only tell them to do what they want to do."

If someone told me what to do and I already wanted to do it, of course I'd follow the suggestion. But how can you want to get up early in the morning to train? And how can you want to train as hard as soldiers do? And how can a soldier want to go into battle knowing that he may get wounded or killed?

The answer is motivation. That general was actually a great motivator. When the wake-up bell was rung in the morning, those soldiers were so motivated that they were probably up already. They really wanted to train and didn't need to be told to. They probably even trained extra!

When it came to going into battle, they were so motivated by patriotism, heroism, or whatever that they couldn't wait for the battle orders to be given. That's the secret of discipline: you're motivated to accept it.

You like getting up early in the morning—you think it's awesome—and you feel disappointed if you sleep in: "Oh! I missed out on something." You want to keep the rules because you see the purpose of it. You're motivated.

I brainwash, I motivate my students, to want to meditate. That's where discipline comes from. If you're a manager or you want to get your kids to do well at school, don't use a stick or shout at them—use other forms of motivation. You get the best discipline when people are motivated to do what's required.

How can the control freak be dealt with? Please explain in detail.

We control because we're afraid to let go. We control because we've been hurt in the past, because we think we need to protect ourselves by planning our future and trying to control the environment. But things still go wrong. In fact, the more we control, the more things go wrong. If you really want to be safe, let go.

The first time I got a bicycle I was about eleven years old. In the beginning I was so afraid of falling off that I grabbed the handlebars until my knuckles went white. Because I was so stiff when I went around a corner, I couldn't balance and kept falling off. However, after a while I just forgot about falling off, and then just played around like young kids do. Once I relaxed, I could ride my bike really fast and there was no problem.

Looking back, I realize that it was fear that caused me to fall off. Fear makes you try to control, and controlling makes you fall. When you understand how this works, you stop being so afraid. Part of this is realizing that it's all right to fail. When you realize that you're allowed to make mistakes, you relax, and then you're not a control freak anymore.

Why are we always controlling? Fear. So let go of fear. What are you afraid of anyway? Don't be afraid of what others think of you. People don't think of you anyway; you're not that important! Just relax and be as stupid as you want. That way you don't have to be a control freak. When there's nothing to be afraid of, you can let go of all control. At last you can be peaceful, and you stop falling off your bicycle!

Is seeing the impermanence of ordinary sense perceptions part of how we become familiar with change and capable of accepting it, so that we can let go in meditation and stop controlling?

Yes. Let's investigate this. For instance, people like different kinds of food. Me, I love fish and chips. I can't understand why everyone doesn't like fish and chips! It's the most delicious food in the whole world! I think it's what we should have every day, for lunch and for breakfast.

But what I like might not be what you like. And sometimes you change your likes. Sometimes you don't want what you normally like. Today you feel like something else. So even your likes change. You can't rely on your sense perceptions.

I had been a monk for about ten years before I got my first hot fish and chips in Australia. As a monk in Thailand, eating such things as frog on rice, sometimes you dreamed of fish and chips.

One day after I'd come to live in Australia, I had to do a funeral service in the early morning, and there wasn't enough time to get back to the monastery for lunch. Ajahn Jagaro, who was the abbot at that time, told me, "Just get something to eat on your way back."

"You mean actually choose something myself?!"

So the anagarika driving me took me to a fish-and-chips shop. For the first time in years I had fish and chips—not with curry and other stuff on top, but just hot fish and chips on a piece of paper, with vinegar and salt. The food we get at the monastery—by the time it arrives and we finish all the chanting—is usually cold. But this time my meal was going to be hot!

This was it! Hot fish and chips! This is what I'd been dreaming about for ten years! But after I ate it, I had a tummy ache! It was such a downer. Why?

My perceptions, when they got tested, didn't live up to their promise.

How many times in life has it been the case that something you've dreamed of, something you've salivated over, was no big deal once you actually got it? Why do we waste so much time wanting things?

Conversely, even if you've had a bad retreat, you might change your perception to regard it as a good one, because you'd feel embarrassed to tell your friends how much money and time you'd wasted. Instead, you say something positive: "I learned a lot on that retreat." You change your perception, based on what you want to tell people—that's why you can't trust your perceptions. They're lies.

Is fear a type of ill will?

Yes, fear is ill will toward losing control, and it disappears when you learn how to let go and you're not afraid of messing up. Confess your mistakes to everyone, get them out in the open, and then you can have a good laugh about them.

Remember, you're allowed to make mistakes. It's OK to fall off the bike. If it's OK, you learn and you don't fall off again. But if you're afraid of making mistakes, afraid of falling off, you make even more mistakes.

I've made that a very important teaching at Bodhinyana Monastery. I say, "Monks, you're allowed to make mistakes." And because they're allowed to make mistakes, they don't make so many. If I was on their back all the time, telling them off every time they did something wrong, they would make heaps more. But when we say: "You can make mistakes. It's OK. I, too, have made mistakes and done stupid things," we create an atmosphere in which people are relaxed, and then they make fewer mistakes. You learn this in meditation.

Today I had a big negative reaction toward someone in my mind. At first, I was surprised and disappointed, because I thought I was in a happy state. This got me thinking about the authenticity of my happy state. Have I just been generating it at the surface level of my mind in the same way I can indulge in a feel-good movie, knowing that the feeling will fade away shortly afterward? I don't know what to think.

Something comes up in your mind? It's par for the course: you're having a happy state and it doesn't last. Look at it this way: without the negative reaction you wouldn't appreciate the happiness. You need to feel the opposite to really appreciate the happiness. If you were happy all the time, you'd just take it for granted, and you wouldn't value it. So this negative reaction was wonderful! Now you can really appreciate the value of happiness. It was a great teaching for you. Welcome it.

One reason to go on retreat is that sometimes at home, because people are already stressed out, they create more stress by reacting in silly ways—by watching too much TV, say, instead of meditating—and then beating themselves up about it. On retreat there's no TV, so you can use your time to strengthen your ability to be at peace, and then when you go home you will have developed the right skills and you won't have to deal with self-created stress. You'll be able to just sit down, make peace with the stress, be kind, be gentle, and the stress, and thus the tendency to indulge in silly habits, will disappear.

Killing "It" with Kindness

I have a severe phobia of certain flying insects and spiders. It's completely irrational, but enough to freak me out. If I'm meditating and they're around, I feel the urge to get rid of them and end up breaking my precepts. Please tell me how to overcome this fear so that I can let the creatures be.

First of all, don't think about it or worry about it. Just do the meditation and make the mind peaceful and calm. My preceptor (Somdet Phra Buddhajahn) told me that he never did much meditation, except as a young monk. At that time he had been meditating somewhere in the jungle, and when he came out of meditation there was a venomous snake curling up in his lap. The snakes in Thailand are very dangerous. If you move, the first thing the snake does is bite you. But even though he knew how dangerous it was, he didn't have the slightest bit of fear. This really surprised him. He then realized that this is what happens in meditation: things you are usually terrified of are no longer terrifying. It's just a snake, that's all. This happens because your mind is very peaceful and calm. Soon that snake slithered away and he got up.

The same thing will happen with your phobia of mosquitoes and spiders. Don't try to deal with the problem yet. Get your mind into some deep meditation—become peaceful, calm, and happy—and then you won't be afraid. The calm will actually start rewiring your brain into overcoming that phobia. So just carry on with the meditation.

When I was in Thailand, there were tarantulas walking on the ceiling, or rather, on the rafters. Sometimes they would fall off the rafters. It was so hot I just had my lower robe on and my chest was bare. They would fall on top of my bare skin! It happened many times, but I wasn't at all scared. It was just tickly, that's all.

Having a tarantula running over your chest was actually quite pleasant! They weren't going to bite you; they were just having a tour around.

If you try to get rid of fear, it gets worse. Once the mind is peaceful, calm, and happy, there's no problem anymore—the calm rewires your brain to get rid of any fear or phobia. When you see a spider or a flying insect going past, you may think, "My goodness, I'm not reacting!" If you just let it be, if you're peaceful and kind, the fear disappears.

Over the past four years, I've been experiencing panic attacks. I meditate every day and practice yoga and tai chi, but I still get panic attacks. I live in fear of them. How do you overcome panic attacks?

A story I tell on every retreat is about a girl who was studying dentistry at Adelaide University. This girl had such bad panic attacks that she was afraid of leaving her bedroom or even getting out of bed. She had been stuck in her house for months at the time. No one could help her, including psychologists and doctors. She called me up because her uncle is a strong supporter of our monastery.

I told her to locate the panic attacks in her body. She said she didn't know where she felt them. I told her to investigate and call me in three or four days' time. I gave her something to do.

Three or four days later she called and said, "It's in the chest area."

"Wonderful," I replied. "Now, describe those panic attacks to me. How does it feel in that area when you have a panic attack?"

She wasn't able to say. I told her to keep investigating and give me another call in three days' time. Again, I was giving her some work to do, asking her to be mindful of the physical sensations associated with the panic attacks.

Three days later, she called me again. I was impressed with her very detailed description of all the sensations associated with her panic attacks. She was a very intelligent girl.

Then I said: "Great, you've established mindfulness of those sensations. Now practice compassion. The next time you have a panic attack, and you feel those sensations coming on, use your hand to massage that area of your chest. If you can't do it, get your boyfriend to do it. I don't think he will mind."

And that's what she did.

After three or four days, she called me again, and said, "I followed your instructions."

"What happened?"

"Whenever I massage the sensations, they disappear," she said.

"What about the panic?" I ventured.

That was the light-bulb moment. She paused, then said, "The panic goes away as well!"

A few weeks later she was out of her bedroom and back to her studies. A brilliant girl, she got first-class honors in dentistry. She married her boyfriend, and I had the honor of performing the blessing ceremony for her at the Sunken Gardens at the University of Western Australia. She even nominated me for Australian of the Year!

Of course I never received that accolade, but I was deeply touched. She said, "You really saved my life. To nominate you was the least I could do." She now lives happily with her husband in Sydney. She's a top dentist with a wonderful life and no more panic attacks.

Now you know how to deal with panic attacks. Most people are not skilled enough to deal directly with the mental stuff. However, every panic attack has associated physical sensations in the body. By becoming aware of the physical sensations, you can deal with those instead. If you relieve the physical part, you find that the emotional part disappears too.

Locate the physical sensations wherever they are and know them so well that you can describe them in detail to another person. You then have mindfulness of those sensations. Then deal with the sensations, generally by massaging them with as much kindness and softness as you possibly can. When the physical counterpart goes, so does the emotion. I've even taught psychologists to teach this to their patients.

Since childhood I've been anxious and tense. As a student at university, it got so bad that I found myself trying to study but being paralyzed with terror. It has been difficult for me to function properly in the world, but your teachings have been an immense support and I wouldn't have the quality of life I have now without them.

Recently I started to help an organization I care about and my anxiety appeared again. I used my practice, but some stressful issues with people have caused a great deal of tension. I'm wondering if I can keep serving this group without breaking down entirely.

What I've noticed is that I want to do things well, but I have a dreadful fear that failure will result in rejection and isolation. I've seen this in my meditation too. I get to the breath, but quickly leave it, for fear that I might not be able to stay with it. Sometimes this stress and tension gives me headaches and makes me irritable.

This is a very common problem. We feel we have to succeed, to meet other people's expectations. At the very least, we have to meet our own expectations, our own goals and standards. That's why I tell students not to "measure" themselves. If you can do that, you can be at peace with yourself, and just allow yourself to be.

If you want to discover a great truth, just go into the forest and look for a perfect tree. You won't find even one. They're leaning to the left, leaning to the right—they're all weird and gnarled and different. That's what makes the forest beautiful. If all the trees were identical and lined up in straight rows, it would look terrible. The so-called imperfections of a forest are what make it beautiful.

It's the same thing with your own imperfections and all the things you think are wrong with you. You should aim to be a person who allows herself to make mistakes, to be imperfect, to mess up from time to time. Just make peace with your defilements and hindrances. That's what meditation teaches you. Wanting to be perfect just creates anxiety.

Look at me. I don't mind if people don't like my jokes; I tell them anyway. That's how I can be at peace with myself. Other people might be afraid: "What if I tell a joke and no one laughs?" That happens to me all the time. They groan.

Do you remember the story from the Saṁyutta Nikāya about the demon who came into the emperor's palace (page 12)? When a demon of a flaw comes into your life, don't say: "Get out of here. You're not supposed to be in here. I'm supposed to be perfect." Instead say: "Welcome monster. I really messed up today." Welcome and be kind to the flaws in your life. And, of course, you know what happens next. The monster gets smaller and smaller until it vanishes completely. There's no problem anymore when you realize that you're allowed to fail, when you realize that you can mess up and make mistakes. You can get rid of the anxiety once you stop trying to be perfect.

I learned this from Ajahn Chah, who never scolded me when I made a mistake. He just laughed his head off!

During my first year in Thailand, Wat Pa Pong was still a very poor monastery. If you wanted a bar of soap, you had to go and ask your teacher. Ajahn Chah had a big water jar where he would keep what people offered him. If you wanted something, and it was there, he would give it to you. If it wasn't there, he would say sorry.

One day I went to ask for a bar of soap. But since I was only beginning to learn Thai, I got the word slightly wrong. The word for soap in Thai is *saboo*, but I said *saparod*—very close, except that *saparod* means "pineapple." So Ajahn Chah heard that I was asking for a pineapple. He looked at me kindly and asked what I wanted a pineapple for, to which I answered, "You know—to wash, to bathe."

I caused him so much happiness for days! He was telling all the visitors that people from London washed their bodies with pineapples—a very strange culture! "You know, in Thailand we use soap to wash, but in the West, they use pineapples! Maybe they are more advanced than us. Maybe we should try that!"

Instead of being scolded and feeling bad about it, I saw that I had made my teacher happy! Isn't that great! If you make a mistake, you're making people happy—so make more mistakes! It would be such a boring world if everyone were perfect. When you think like this, there's no more anxiety.

When you meditate, your anxiety vanishes because you're just sitting and letting things be, not trying to get anywhere. If you fall asleep, you fall asleep. If you start snoring, that's fine. If other people don't like it, they can get earplugs, and you can just carry on. That way you don't really care what other people think of you and you can have a peaceful time. You don't have to be perfect. "Oh, what a great relief on the spiritual journey of life to realize I don't have to be perfect! I can be free now!"

The alternative is to spend this life, and other lives as well, striving for perfection, for something you can never reach, eventually realizing how stupid you've been. You don't need to strive to be perfect. Let go—that's good enough.

How do I solve the problem of negative thoughts? Even though I'm trying to let go and do mettā meditation, negative thoughts still come up. If we welcome and are kind to our mind and to such thoughts, what happens if our mind starts to follow the distraction? Do we try to control our mind? Also, if someone is angry at us or is trying to manipulate us, how should we react?

Second question first. If it's during a retreat, just forget about what other people are doing. Be an island unto yourself, as the Buddha said, a refuge unto yourself (DN 16). Other people can get angry with you, but that has nothing to do with you. It's their problem, not yours.

Once you leave the retreat, it's a bit more difficult because there are so many angry people in the world. If anger comes your way, just let it go, let it wash right over you. Be like a lotus flower, that symbol of Buddhism. If you urinate on a lotus flower, the urine just flows off it; it leaves no residue and it doesn't smell. If you pour perfume on a lotus, that also just rolls off the petals and leaves no smell. This is because a lotus doesn't retain any residue.

Imagine yourself to be like a lotus. It doesn't matter whether people get angry at you, curse you, or call you all sorts of bad names. Nor does it matter if they say you're the best monk since the time of the Buddha, that you're such a wonderful teacher, etc. Whatever they do or say, it all flows off, and you're still the same "lotus" you were before. You keep nothing, no residue from the past. That's how to react when people are angry at you or try to manipulate you. In the end, they just can't.

Now let's talk about the first question, about the problem with the negative thoughts. If you're negative to the negative thoughts, it's double negativity. Next you get negative about the negativity to the negative thoughts, and it becomes triple negativity! And it goes on and on and on like that until you go crazy!

If you've got a negative thought in your mind, just let it be, embrace it: "Welcome, Negative Thought."

See how negative you can be. See if you can get into the Guinness

Book of Records for the most negative thought ever. If you have a negative thought, laugh at it. If it becomes a bit of a joke, it's not negativity anymore. If you're kind to the negative thoughts and don't buy into them, if you just leave them alone or laugh at them, after a while they just disappear.

CRIMES AND MISDEMEANORS

Please talk about the benefits of right speech and not gossiping.

Four priests were at a conference. At lunch they sat down together and at a pause in the conversation one of the priests made an announcement.

"Friends, I have a secret I want to confess. I watch horseracing. I also go to the casino—I put on dark glasses and a wig. I'm a gambler."

The other priests were taken aback. "That's amazing!" they said. "We thought you were such a pure person! But it's good you told us. When you have a bad character trait, it's good to confess to people you trust. Confession is good for you."

Another priest stood up. "I want to confess too. On Mondays, on my day off, I go to the bottle shop. By Monday evening I'm drunk on whiskey. I'm an alcoholic."

"Whoa!" said the others. "You've hidden it so well! It's a shameful thing for a priest to do, but it's great you've confessed."

Then they asked the third priest, "What's your vice?"

"I can't tell you," he said, sharply.

"Oh, come on," the others said soothingly. "It will be good for you to tell."

The priest took a deep breath. "OK," he said, "There's a girl who comes to my church—she's married, and we're having an affair."

"Ohhh!" they replied in shock. A priest committing adultery! But in support they said: "It's good you told us. Now we can help you."

Then they addressed the fourth priest: "What about you?"

The fourth priest was silent. He sat motionless, eyes cast down toward the floor.

The priests exchanged looks. They were concerned for their friend. Trying to lighten the mood, they joked, "It can't be worse than gambling, drinking, or adultery!"

There was a long pause.

"It's much worse than that," the fourth priest said.

After some time, one of the priests bravely ventured, "What is it, friend?"

"My problem is . . . I'm a gossip. Whatever I hear, I have to tell everybody."

Now you know why you shouldn't gossip! It's worse than gambling, worse than drinking, worse than adultery! So don't do it.

If we feel irritated with someone, is it because we're still not compassionate enough to accept that person totally? If we get irritated and tell someone off, should we make peace with that person or just let go in our meditation? If we are compassionate enough to accept people as they are, does this mean we don't criticize them and that they can just continue doing whatever they're doing wrong?

Being irritated with another person isn't a crime—it's just life. We all irritate one another! I irritate people by telling bad jokes. You irritate others by coughing. Perhaps you irritate your teacher by not getting jhāna—after all those years he's been teaching you! We're all irritating. So the first thing to understand is that just as you feel irritated by others, they also feel irritated by you. In this way you depersonalize it, and you understand that this is what life is like. This means that the most compassionate thing you can do is to get enlightened and not get reborn again. Then there's one less irritating person around! Irritation is part of life. Don't expect anything else.

Ajahn Chah told a great story about a farmer who had a chicken, and he wanted it to be a duck. End of story.

Does that make sense to you? You've got a boyfriend, and you want him to be "just like this." He's a chicken, but you want him to be a duck. You've got a girlfriend, and you want her to be so beautiful. But if she's a duck, she can't be a chicken. You need to accept people for who they are. Dogs are dogs, and they bark; crows are crows, and they go "caw, caw, caw"; mosquitoes are mosquitoes and go "bzzz bzzz bzzz," and then they bite you!

Why do we get irritated by things that are just being what they're supposed to be? Instead of wanting the world to be different, accept it as it is. Asking from the world what it can never give you is suffering. Can you ask other people not to be irritating? You can ask, but you'll never get the answer you want. People are irritating. Husbands are suffering.

The only thing that isn't suffering is the teddy bear that sits in the meditation hall at the monastery. He just sits there perfectly still, never asking a question. He never complains. He must have been enlightened a long time ago!

Teddy bears are teddy bears. When you understand what people are, you never ask them for what they can't give you. You can never ask people, even in your heart, to be perfectly silent. They can't do that, nor can you. That's why you just let this world be.

Irritation is asking for what you can't get—from yourself, from your partner, from your friends, from life. When you realize what life can give you and what it can't, you don't get irritated anymore. You don't criticize, and you just have fun.

How does one reconcile letting go of control with trying to prevent someone from harming others or even from doing self-harm? For example, a monk who reportedly had sex, or a person in a powerful position in the workplace who is bullying or victimizing people who need their jobs too badly to stand up to him.

Controlling is usually not the answer. The best thing is to be kind and do your duties to make sure other people are happy. Controlling is demanding that the outcome will be just as you want it.

A lot of the time, when you try to stop people, you just can't. It's beyond your power. You can give it a try and see what happens. If it works, fine. But if you try to control and you can't achieve your goal, you get frustrated. When you get frustrated, you get angry. After you get angry, you get depressed. A lot of depressed people are angry at the world and angry at themselves. They have failed to control things. They have wasted so much energy, resulting in a low energy state, in depression. They're burned out, fighting battles they can never win.

Loving-kindness is trying your best, but always having equanimity waiting in the wings in case it doesn't work. A good example is the work of a doctor. What's a doctor's main job? It's not to cure—that's controlling. The job of a doctor is to care. Trying to cure patients often results in failure. And just before the failure, the doctor gets frustrated. The doctor then intervenes in all sorts of unnecessary and unpleasant ways, desperately trying to keep the patient alive. This happens because curing is the doctor's number-one priority. If the top priority is caring, there comes a time when the doctor can let her patient die. Instead of thinking she has to keep her patient alive at all costs, she cares for him in his final moments. If caring becomes the number-one priority for doctors, a lot of people will die far more peacefully.

Trying to cure people is being a control freak. Trying to cure your spouse or yourself of your bad habits, or trying to control the defilements and hindrances in meditation—it's endless. It doesn't work. Instead, care for yourself.

When you care for your mind, the defilements vanish by themselves. When you try to control, they get worse. Don't try to cure your stupidity. Care for it. Kindness works, controlling doesn't. Controlling promises success, but all that you'll get is frustration. It's by caring that you reach the goal. The problems disappear and you're at peace.

How can you train yourself not to judge other people?

If you do judge other people, don't worry about it; don't judge yourself for judging others!

Think about it: How can you judge other people? What do you really know about them? If you could read their minds, if you knew their whole history and exactly why they did what they did, then maybe you could judge them. But you can only have incomplete information, which makes you just jump to conclusions.

Many years ago, at a time when many monks in Thailand were caught with mistresses, I decided to make a confession before a large crowd at our Dhammaloka Centre in Perth. I said, in front of many loyal supporters, with perfect honesty, that I had spent some of the happiest moments of my life in the loving arms of another man's wife. We kissed, we hugged, we loved each other.

People were shocked! They judged me. They said: "Oh, no! Not Ajahn Brahm too!" Then I told them that the woman was my mother. It was the truth. As a young child, I'd had some of the happiest moments of my life in the loving arms of my mother. And she was definitely another man's wife. Once I had explained, they said, "Oh, yeah, that's OK."

They had assumed I had committed adultery as a monk. I had succeeded in tricking them. I wanted to demonstrate how easy it is to judge someone incorrectly, even when you have all the facts right.

Have you ever been judged incorrectly, accused of something you didn't do? It has happened to me many times. But that's life. Even the Buddha was judged for things he didn't do. We need to realize that this is just normal.

This is why we should always give others the benefit of the doubt. If your husband comes home late from work, assume it's because he was working overtime. Don't judge him and assume he was with another woman.

Years ago, we went to meet Ajahn Nyanadhammo at the airport. When he came out, he smelled like a distillery! We asked him what the heck he'd been doing. His said that on the flight from Adelaide to Perth he'd been sitting next to a man who was terrified of flying. The only way he could cope with the anxiety was by drinking glass after glass of whiskey. As they were coming in to land at Perth airport, there was turbulence, and as a result the man spilled a full glass of whiskey over Ajahn Nyanadhammo's robe. That was his explanation, and we gave him the benefit of the doubt.

It's not nice to judge people. If you're tempted to judge, please remember that the other person is innocent until proven guilty beyond reasonable doubt.

From time to time I experience a fleeting feeling of dissatisfaction. What could be the cause? What's a skillful way to manage it?

Only a fleeting feeling? If it's a fleeting feeling, it goes by itself. Be satisfied that your dissatisfaction is fleeting! It's just the way your mind is; let it go. If it's only a short dissatisfaction, that's wonderful: two bad bricks in the wall make the wall beautiful.

If you have a little bit of dissatisfaction in life, you can really appreciate life the rest of the time. If you were satisfied all the time, you'd take it for granted. According to Christian theology, anyone who goes to heaven has to go to hell one day a year to better appreciate heaven. Otherwise heaven would be taken for granted. That's actually quite a profound understanding. So, having a little bit of dissatisfaction in life enables you to appreciate the peace more.

Today, sitting in the secret garden, I joyfully slapped dead the mosquito that had been biting me. Just as I pondered the rightness of killing, the door of your cottage opened, and there stood a kind and generous monk.

If you want to know why we shouldn't kill mosquitoes, ask the mosquitoes. The mosquitoes will tell you: "I'm too young to die! I've got a life! I don't want to die yet!"

Do mosquitoes want to die? Are they suicidal? Do you reckon they just come and say: "Kill me, please. Please squash me. I really want to be squashed." Or do they fly away if they realize they're going to be squashed? The reason we don't kill is that animals are afraid of death, just like you. Imagine big beings with big hands, squashing you like a mosquito. Would that be fun? So be careful.

I'm married but have romantic feelings and thoughts about a colleague. I notice a pleasure in the fantasy, but I realize that it's a waste of time. Help! What are the karmic consequences of adultery?

The karmic consequences of adultery are terrible! Oh, terrible! You lose all your money, the lawyers get everything, and it's just a waste of time.

Fantasizing about someone is the fun part, whether it's a work colleague or casual acquaintance. But please don't take fantasies seriously, because they are not true to reality. If you run away with your colleague, say, you'll be terribly disappointed. In fantasyland, we make the object of our desire up to be whatever we like, and an ordinary person becomes Angelina Jolie. But when you find out that that's not the reality, you'll be so disappointed. Do you want to get into trouble for that? Fantasies are just exaggerations of the real world. They're not reality. So don't buy into them.

I have enough experience, even though I've never been married. All husbands, all men, are exactly the same. Don't think that your colleague is somehow different from the man you've already got. You might think, "My husband is boring, but this man is really interesting." After some time, it'll be: "Here we go again, just like my husband! No better!" It's the same with women. They may have a different chassis, but the engine is the same. So stick with the one you've got. It's much cheaper!

How do we face unkind people or those who just pretend to be good? I meet such people at work.

Easy, don't go back to work. Ordain as a monk or a nun and live at the monastery!

People who are unkind to others are unkind to themselves. A long time ago a wise person said, in reference to working with such people: "You only have to endure them for eight or nine hours a day, five days a week. They have to endure themselves twenty-four hours a day, seven days a week, for the rest of their lives." It must be painful for them to live with themselves if that's how they treat others. When you think like that, it gives rise to compassion. Unkind people must have a terrible life.

I gave a talk one day about right speech. Whenever you use wrong speech, it depresses you. You get the karmic response straightaway. If you shout at someone, curse her, or get negative toward him, it really hurts you and brings you down. Always saying cruel and critical things to other people is one of the reasons people are depressed. If you change your speech—always praising people, being kind to them, and smiling at them—whether it affects other people or not, it certainly affects you. When I praise someone I feel good. When I criticize someone, I just lose my energy. If it's really right speech, you get a big energy boost.

If you meet unkind people, think of how low their energy must be and the black space they must be living in. Then you can be compassionate toward them rather than return their unkindness. Otherwise you get dragged down to their level. So develop compassion toward unkind people at your workplace and always say nice things to them.

What should lay people do about misbehaving monks? In Thailand, an abbot of a temple was having sex with a woman on a regular basis. The other monks at the temple were also misbehaving. The villagers were aware of the situation but continued to support them, even giving alms food, reasoning that they were supporting the Sangha, not just those specific monks. One monk even said: "The villagers know that monks should be good. But good monks are rare. Although those monks are bad, they keep the Sangha going."

Unfortunately, there are bad monks in all countries, and they give Buddhism a bad name. Those laypeople were not supporting the Sangha. If a monk has sex, he has to disrobe straightaway. He's not a monk anymore. By giving requisites to such a monk, you aren't supporting the Sangha—you're destroying it.

If a monk wants to have sex—which would break one of his most basic precepts—he should disrobe and get married like everyone else. Regarding monks who have sex, the Buddha said, "It's better for you to eat a red-hot ball of iron or to put your male organ into the mouth of a snake." In this case, the Buddha was quite fierce.

When I read that I thought, "Oh my goodness, I'd better not do anything wrong!"

Those villagers should have been told that they were doing the wrong thing if they wanted to protect the Sangha. Or the local authority should have been brought in to investigate the issue. Marrying and starting a family is fine—as long as you're not a monk.

Positive Reinforcement

You have said that the positive energy of one person can flow to another, in particular after meditation. Does it work the same way with negative energy? For example, I spent Christmas with my folks, who are very negative, particularly when they get together. After four days, I too became negative, and I couldn't wait to get out of there. What I'm concerned about is this: if we inherit such qualities, do we get stuck with negative traits?

It must be in your genes to be negative! No, it has nothing to do with your genes. It's true that if you hang around positive people, you do get positive energy. And if you hang around negative people, it's easy to get negative energy. That's why it's so great to be on retreat. You hang out with good people, even with monks and nuns. And solitude in its own right is good for building up positive energy.

Anyway, you just have to try to be positive, and then you can give a lot of positive energy to your parents. When you run out of positive energy, give your parents a CD of Dhamma talks to listen to.

My parents were actually very good. I talk a lot about my father because he was a very kind and wise man. Interestingly, my dad would never say much about my grandfather, his own dad, who died during the Second World War. One day—I must have been about thirteen or fourteen—I really pressed my dad: "Why don't you talk about my grandfather? I'd like to know who he was and what he did."

My father said, "Your grandfather, my father, was a bastard."

And I thought: "My goodness! Why is he saying that about his father?"

And then my father let on what had happened. My grandfather was a plumber in Liverpool during the Depression, and money was very tight. Whatever money he earned, he spent at the pub, and he came home drunk every night. Coming home drunk, he took off his leather belt and whipped anyone who came into his path for no reason whatsoever. And he'd lay into his wife, my father's mother. It was gross domestic abuse, which was not uncommon in those days.

But my father said, "Whenever I was at the end of a whipping with that belt"—he had done nothing wrong; it was just that his father was drunk—"I made a resolution: 'If I ever make it through this and I have children, I'll never ever do that to my kids.'"

And he never did. He couldn't discipline us at all! To discipline us was to be reminded of what had happened to him.

Sometimes people think that a victim of sexual or physical abuse will revisit that abuse on their children. It doesn't always work that way, as the example of my own father shows. Instead, he turned it around. He learned from the pain to be a very kind, loving man. It can be done.

That's the lesson in the story about digging in the dog poo in my book *Who Ordered This Truckload of Dung?* Fertilize the mango tree with the poo, and your mangoes become sweeter and juicier than ordinary mangoes! That was my father—he dug it in. He didn't revisit abuse on his children, but learned from it. Good on him!

I'm stupid. I can't react appropriately even in a positive and lovely environment such as a retreat provides. And I can't react fast enough to say no when I don't want to do something. Sometimes it causes a lot of misunderstanding with other people. How can I forgive myself for being too stupid or too slow? Sometimes my mind just goes blank.

Your mind is blank? Brilliant. You are peaceful and still. Stupid people can get into jhāna much more quickly than intelligent ones.

Here's a story I love telling: There was a Thai boy in a rural area who was in grade 1 in his local school. After a year in grade 1, his teacher had to fail him. While all his friends went on to grade 2, he had to repeat grade 1.

After another year in grade 1, he failed again. He was given one more chance. But after three years in grade 1, he still wasn't ready for grade 2, and he had to leave school. Imagine being kicked out of school after grade 1—that qualifies for the Guinness Book of Records for utter stupidity!

What to do with someone so stupid? He was sent to the local temple to be ordained as a novice! (But not all novices start out that way!)

The abbot of the village monastery was very kind and patient with him, much more so than his schoolteachers had been. He tried to teach him some simple chanting like *Namo tassa*: "*Namo*. . . . What was the second word again? Oh, yeah, *tassa*. Now, what was the first word?"

His mind was so blank he couldn't even remember *Namo tassa*, let alone all the other chants most monks have to do. After three years, the abbot also gave up on him. So, what do you think happened? As the last resort, this stupid boy was sent to a forest monastery. Because he couldn't chant or study, he was taught meditation: "Just watch your breath go in and out." His mind was so clear and simple that he could do that for hours. He got into the jhānas, and became fully enlightened. Later he became a famous monk.

Now there was a guy who was totally stupid. If you're stupid, you have a lot of potential!

Can you talk about the accumulated energy in an established meditation center and how one senses it?

It's amazing how people who are normally insensitive to such things can be deeply affected by the energy in certain places.

One of the people at our city center, who used to be a Christian, had helped for many years with the bookkeeping. Her husband was a Buddhist, and after a while, she too became a devout Buddhist. Her husband wanted to go on a pilgrimage that I was leading to the Buddhist holy sites in India, and so she tagged along.

Before we left, I gave an orientation to all going on the pilgrimage. I mentioned that some of the places we'd be going to had very powerful energy. The woman thought I was crazy. She was born in England, and she'd been to many old castles and palaces where kings and queens had lived centuries ago. "What do you mean?" she thought. "It's just old stones, that's all. It's history. Nothing more than that."

The very first place she went was the Mahābodhi Temple in Bodh

Gaya. Afterward she came to ask me for forgiveness. She told me that as soon as she had walked into that temple, totally unexpectedly, she started weeping. Not crying, but weeping and weeping. She couldn't stop herself. It touched her so deeply.

These places have amazing energy. You may go there and think it's just where the Buddha became enlightened, so what? But it's really got power.

You just can't stop yourself from feeling it. I've told many people that when I go to Vulture Peak, where the Buddha spent a lot of time in solitude, it gets to me every time—I just start crying. You get this incredible energy—this inspiration, this happiness. This is where the Buddha meditated a lot. It's got huge energy and power.

On one pilgrimage to India, before the airport at Bodh Gaya had been built, we landed in Kathmandu. We started with a tour of the city. I was bored because it was all about palaces and places of historical and architectural interest. Nothing really fascinated me. I wasn't following the tour guide anymore, but was being rebellious and having a look around by myself. As we were going past a palace, I went through a doorway into a courtyard. My goodness! The energy there was so bad! So negative! So black! It was so bad that I left pretty quickly. I asked the tour guide what that place was. He said it was where the king slaughtered animals for the annual Hindu festival. I had just wandered in there, not knowing what it was. But now I understood. Just to imagine all those animals being ritually killed every year. That place was horrible. It was a terrible place. You just wanted to get out straightaway.

That's what I mean by places having energy. That's why in meditation centers like ours we build up this very supportive energy. At Jhana Grove we're still building it up, but in other places the energy is already huge.

GOING GENTLY INTO THAT GOOD NIGHT

Little by little my mind is calming down and getting rid of depression, but during the night I have terrible nightmares related to my depression issues.

When you go to bed at night, condition your mind before you go to sleep: "May all beings be happy and well. May all beings be free from suffering. May the whole world be at peace." If you have beautiful thoughts as you go to sleep, you'll have beautiful dreams, if you dream at all. And you'll have a good rest. So do a bit of positive reinforcement just before you fall asleep.

Or, I'm a bit embarrassed about this, but it apparently works: you can listen to my talks, and that will send you to sleep. It's a bit of a downer when people say, "I use your talks to go to sleep at night!" But if they have a peaceful sleep, I suppose that's good. You can try it. Get some copies of my talks and play them to yourself in bed, and then you might have a peaceful sleep. But you may have a nightmare about the jokes! Seriously, try one of my talks. It will provide positive input before you fall asleep, and it may even help to prevent bad dreams or nightmares. You deserve a good night's sleep.

Can we use meditation to replace sleep at night?

Yes. I often see my students falling asleep while they're meditating!

If you're meditating properly and very deeply, you get so peaceful and still that you don't need to sleep at night. The whole purpose of sleep is to rest the brain. When the brain has been resting during the day, you don't need to sleep at night. If a car hasn't been out of the garage, it doesn't need any gas.

When your meditation is really peaceful and you go to bed, you don't sleep—you just rest the body. You're totally mindful and aware for three or four hours, and then you get up and carry on meditating. And you never have any bad side effects. You're just peaceful and happy, with lots of energy.

But don't force it. Don't say, "I'm going to stay up all night." Instead, just carry on meditating when everything is energetic and peaceful, and before you know it it'll be dawn. That's the natural way. Don't go without sleep as an act of will, torturing yourself. If you really need to sleep, the body will tell you, and you should act accordingly.

> Giving without asking for anything in return, having a pure heart, is what letting go in meditation is about. You learn to give your energy to the moment without expecting anything in return—not nimittas, or jhāna, or anything—and you purify your heart while you're doing so.

6.

Beyond the Incense Smoke

Bowing, scraping, and gifting does not a Buddhist make.

The best way you can thank teachers is to make them happy. I become happy when my students get into a deep meditation, when their life becomes peaceful and smooth, when they get into some real bliss. I love teaching when people say, "Oh, Ajahn Brahm, the meditation is so nice!" Eventually it happens. To see students blissed out and happy, that's payback for me—that's why I do what I do.

The Buddha said the way to show him gratitude wasn't merely by offering flowers, candles, and incense and by chanting. You pay proper respect to the Buddha by following his teachings and by achieving peace and happiness.

And how do you say thank you to your parents for all they've done for you? You say it by being a happy and good son or daughter. That's all parents want for their children, and that's the greatest gift you can give them.

Can you please explain why we bow three times at the end of your talks?

It's because we need to exercise our stomachs. Otherwise we'll put on weight.

Well, perhaps not. The truth of the matter is that whenever I bow, I bow to what the Buddha represents.

The first thing I put my head down to is virtue. I bow to virtue because virtue—goodness, trustworthiness—is really important to me. I love living with virtuous people, and they don't come more virtuous than monks, nuns, and anagarikas. I worship virtue, and that's what I bow to first of all.

The second time I bow to peace—peace in my heart, peace in meditation, peace in the community, peace in the world. Peace is something I find very easy to worship.

Lastly, I bow to compassion and kindness. Every time I see an act of kindness or compassion it brightens up the world. It creates so much happiness, joy, and hope.

In this way, I remember these three things every time I bow. It's like jogging my memory: "Ajahn Brahm, virtue is really important. I bow to that. Peace is really important. I bow to that. Compassion is gorgeous. I bow to that." Every time I bow I remember and reinforce the importance of virtue, peace, and compassion.

If you like the idea, I encourage you to do the same. If there are other qualities you really venerate, remember those when you bow. It's a beautiful way to reinforce those qualities, and it helps to make them grow inside you.

Why do we chant?

A bit of chanting gives you some helpful teachings. Take the *Mettā Sutta*: "Let them be able and upright." "Upright" means not sleeping so much. When you sleep you're not upright, you're horizontal.

In the suttas the animals are called *tiracchānagata*, which literally means "beings that go horizontally." We go vertically, but animals go horizontally. So if you spend too much time being horizontal in your life, you may be reborn as a horizontal being, because that's what you're used to.

There are lots of beautiful phrases in the *Mettā Sutta*, such as, "Let them be contented and easily satisfied, not proud and demanding in nature." Now that's a teaching about how to meditate. Be contented. Be easily satisfied with your meditation. Don't be proud, wanting to be the best meditator. Don't be demanding. Don't ask for more. Even when you get just a little bit of peace, you think: "Thank you so much, this is such a great gift. This is good enough for me." Don't demand anything from your meditation. Just be happy to have the opportunity to close your eyes and be at peace. Anything else is just extra.

If you're demanding or if you've got goals, you think: "I have to get nimittas by the end of my retreat or I'm going to ask for my money back. I'm not going to be contented. It's a great sacrifice taking time off work, giving a lot of money, spending money on plane tickets and everything else. I demand value for money, at least jhāna!" That's not being contented and easily satisfied. It's being proud and demanding. That's not kindness, love, or peace, nor is it mettā. You'll never get deep meditation that way.

When you meditate, don't demand anything of yourself or your mind. Don't expect your body to be free from pain. Instead, be content: "Thank you, body, for just being able to sit for a few minutes." If that's your attitude, your meditation takes off. You get very peaceful and very still.

The chanting has a lot of meaning to it. What I've just explained is only a little bit. When you chant, it's another form of brainwashing.

Get Ritual or Get Real

Can we take the three refuges and eight precepts with the morning chanting?

Once you've taken the refuges, that's it—just keep them in your heart. The same goes for the precepts. You can chant them and chant them and chant them, but keeping them is what's important.

Too many people in traditional Buddhist countries take the precepts every time they go to the temple, but have a bottle of whiskey waiting in the trunk of their car. It's just an empty ceremony for so many. So keep the precepts instead of always taking them. That's what's important.

Where I come from, Buddhism often gets mixed up with Taoism, which has lots of rituals. As a result, many people think Buddhism is

all superstition, which is why they think it is cooler to be a Christian than a Buddhist.

In the West, being a Buddhist is really cool. One day I was walking past the hardware store in Armadale, a low socioeconomic area, and some kids straight out of high school—"yobbos," we used to call them—came up to me and asked: "Are you a Buddhist monk? A *real* Buddhist monk?"

"Yes," I replied.

And they said, "Cool!"

There are many rituals in Buddhism, but there are many in Christianity as well. There's much superstition in all religions. Some practices are quite innocent, and some have their origins in the local cultures.

But sometimes the rituals are so thick in Buddhist temples that you can't see the Buddha statue for the incense smoke. You can't see the Dhamma, the teachings, because of all the rituals you have to do before you can listen to a talk or find a monk. That's why in my monastery we try to strip away as many rituals as possible.

For example, the ritual of all-night *paritta* chanting (reciting certain verses and scriptures for protection) goes against what the Buddha said we should do. It's prohibited in the Vinaya (the monastic regulations). But what do people do? They get monks to chant all night, thinking it will make them lots of merit. Usually they chant just three suttas, such as the *Mettā Sutta*. To make it last all night, they bring their palms together in *añjali* mudra and go, "Naaaaaaa-aaa-aaaaaa-aaaaa-aaaaaaa-aaaaaa-aaaaaaa-aa moooooooooo-oooooooo. . . ." So slow.

That's stupid! But because your parents and grandparents did it, you're too scared to stop that. Sometimes it's just the fear of offending someone.

And what about lighting all those paper houses and stuff? Where does that smoke go? Does it go to heaven? No, it goes about twenty-five feet up and then blows all over the city. It never gets to heaven. Heaven is not *up* there.

Some of these rituals and rites really need to be challenged. I've heard that in some temples in Singapore menstruating women are not allowed to enter. That's ridiculous! Nuns live in temples seven days a week. Some of these rituals are so ridiculous that they actually give Buddhism a bad name.

This was my first retreat, and it was a mind-blowingly positive experience. I was born and raised a Buddhist, but it took this retreat for me to realize the true meaning of Buddhism. If the Buddha realized the truth and became so wise, years ago, then what on earth have human beings been doing for so long?

People just bow to statues, instead of listening to the teachings of the Buddha. That's one of the problems in traditional Buddhist countries. You can't get close to the real teachings that way; it's all just rituals.

David Blair, a professor of physics at the University of Western Australia, went to Thailand when he was young because of his interest in Buddhism. But he couldn't ask any questions: it was all just chanting, rituals, bowing, and offering of food to monks. No one would actually give him the real teachings.

So I coined a metaphor to describe much of what passes for Buddhism in many Asian countries: You can't see the Buddha for the incense smoke. There's so much incense and other stuff that you can't see the real Buddha through it all. That's what humans have been doing. They've made too much of a religion around Buddhism, and few understand what the Buddha actually taught.

It's the same reason there's corruption in ostensibly Buddhist countries: Buddhism has been reduced to rituals, and its real meaning has been lost.

Take the five precepts. When you take the five precepts, you're not supposed to drink any alcohol. However, when you go to countries like Sri Lanka and Thailand and Burma, you see wine shops all over the place and people getting drunk. It didn't use to be that way. Often the ceremonies are all that remain, and people have lost respect for the true religion. For a lot of people, it's just a matter of going to the temple and offering food or money, almost like a bribe to somehow wipe out the bad *kamma* they did the night before. That's not Buddhism; that's ritual.

A lot of it is actually the laypeople's fault for supporting bad monks and for building huge temples with lots of gold. And what for? Because you think that's making merit. There is tons of bottled water at our monastery. Want to know why?

About ten years ago a general in Thailand dreamed that his dead father came to him. His father told him that he was getting food and clothes where he was now, because his son had been giving those things to the temple, but that he wasn't getting anything to drink! The father asked his son to offer water, too. The general told the public about his dream, and now Thai people who offer food to monks offer bottled water as well. Our monastery gets heaps and heaps of bottled water. I keep telling them that we've got nice rainwater in the taps, but it doesn't make much difference.

Here's another little story about how not to make merit. Awhile back somebody gave me a big bucket of requisites as an offering for his dead father, and hidden inside the bucket was a small bottle of whiskey! And I received it! I didn't know about it, but later on the anagarikas found it. I asked that layperson why he did that. He told me that his father had liked whiskey and that if he didn't give some to the monks, his father wouldn't get any whiskey in heaven!

That's the stupidity of some people. What you offer to the monks is not what your father gets in heaven. Just do good and share the merits; that's enough.

Those who are not stupid sometimes turn away from Buddhism. They become atheists because they can't see the purpose of being a Buddhist. A major reason for this is that many Buddhist temples are corrupt. The monks live luxurious lives in big temples, instead of living in simple accommodations. Anyone who comes to Bodhinyana Monastery is welcome to go inside my "residence." It's a small cave. And I sleep on the floor even though I'm a famous senior monk. It's a good example to others. We don't need expensive stuff. You won't find any TVs in Bodhinyana Monastery; we live very simply. And that gives inspiration. It would be wonderful if there were more monks and nuns living the simple life in Buddhist countries—that would provide sorely needed inspiration in our modern world.

Medication versus Mettā-tation

I heard you once helped a young girl recover from depression. Do you think there's any usefulness in antidepressants or medication, or can meditation alone cure depression, even in severe cases?

For very severe cases of depression, people sometimes need medication, and even sessions with a psychologist or a psychiatrist. But for the average depression—the majority of cases—meditation works. And it's a wonderful way to overcome it.

Depression is just low mental energy. When you try to fight it, you're just wasting more energy and you become even more depressed. You literally get depressed about being depressed. Every time you fight, you go deeper into dullness and negativity.

The opposite of that is meditation. "Welcome depression," you say to it. "I love being depressed because there are many benefits: I don't have to get up in the morning, and I've got a great excuse for not going to work." When you're depressed other people look after you. They care for you, and they try to cheer you up. You don't have to perform. So enjoy it!

What I'm saying is that if you don't fight, but instead open the door of your heart to your depression, you build positive energy, and the depression gradually goes away. Fight it, and it gets worse. Love it, and it shrinks. It's a hard thing to do, but it works.

I have a boyfriend who has a quick and strong temper. He's trying to change, but he's refused to do meditation despite our having arguments over this. How can he improve his awareness? Should I change boyfriends?

Yes, there are many boyfriends around; get a good one. If you had a microwave that didn't work, would you change it?

Of course you would. Your boyfriend must be a faulty model; take him back to the manufacturer and get a refund.

Should I force him to meditate, or should I let go of any hope that he will change and do nothing?

If you're a smart girl, you'll realize that you have what I call leverage over your boyfriend. You have the power to persuade him. If he starts to go to the temple and meditate, be nice to him, be kind. That's called positive reinforcement. And it works. So use your leverage.

I'm scared of lizards. I've seen the same species three times today. I realize that I should have mettā for them, but when I close my eyes

and try to say, "May the lizards be happy," I'm so scared that I can't continue with the meditation. Is it true that if you're scared of something, you shouldn't include it in your mettā meditation?

Those stumpy-tailed lizards are so harmless, you can pick them up. Even schoolchildren do. Those lizards are lovely animals. They're perfectly safe and they won't do anything to you. Most of the time they're just doing what they need to—walking around and having a good time. If they come into the hall, it's because they want to do some meditation.

If you're scared of anything, do some research and find out if it is really worth being scared of it. Knowledge is the first thing that overcomes fear. Once you've got some knowledge, it'll change your state of mind. No one has ever been bitten by a lizard here. Give mettā to your fear, whether it's a lizard or an ant or whatever.

Love and mettā come from nonself. As soon as there's a self, a "me" or a "mine," there's controlling, and you can't let go. When there's no self, there's no controlling, and you can accept people as they are. That's when love and mettā are truly possible. When "you" disappear, mettā is what's left. The more "you" there is, the less mettā there is. So butt out, and let mettā take over!

I'm a working mother. How can I find time to meditate when I have so many chores to attend to? Is it good to go to the gym with loud music when we start practicing meditation? What are the drawbacks if we do?

If you're a working mother, you really need to meditate; otherwise you'll be a pain in the neck for your kids. Ask your kids. Many working mothers come to our meditation classes.

At one time in our Armadale meditation group, a woman told us after the meditation that she hadn't felt like coming that evening because she had been so busy all day. But then her kid said, "Mummy, are you going to meditation today?"

"No darling, I'm tired," she said.

"Mummy, you must go to meditation."

"I don't feel like it."

"Mummy, please go to meditation!"

"Why?"

"Because you're a much nicer mummy afterward!"

And that's why she went! Many other mothers have told me similar stories. The kids know their mothers are stressed out, and when they're stressed out they're no fun. So mothers should go to meditation for the sake of their kids.

You can go to the gym—it's not one or the other. There's some interesting wisdom by Ajahn Chah: "If you want a healthy body, you have to exercise it. If you want a healthy mind, you have to keep it still."

When you get to my age, you may think, "Oh my goodness, I have to do Sudoku puzzles, or I'll get dementia!" We think we have to exercise or our brain will disappear. But stillness gives you a far healthier and stronger brain than doing puzzles. That was one of Ajahn Chah's brilliant insights: "If you want a healthy mind, keep it still."

Can you suggest a good way to teach meditation to a small child? My daughter is four and never sits still.

Straitjacket!

No, really, if you want the kid to meditate, the best thing is for you to meditate. If you meditate, the kid will sit next to you, and sometimes kids pick up on the parent's energy. If you're really frantic and just all over the place, then the kid will become frantic. If you're peaceful, the kid will be, too. Kids learn by osmosis.

Can you please explain in scientific terms how meditation gives you the supernatural ability to predict the future and look into the past lives of others?

I can predict the future because I've got very good meditation—the future is, and I always get it right, uncertain!

No one can predict the future. The only thing anyone knows about the future for sure is that each of us is going to die. That's my prediction. That's about as far as anyone can go. Someone who says she can predict the future is a fraud.

Regarding past lives, you can only look into your own. You can only know the past lives of others if you happened to be there together with them. That's as far as you can go.

There was once a king who had a minister in his court who was a real smart aleck. He always knew everything about other people, and he would always upset them.

One day the other ministers decided to bring him down. This was their plan: they would praise him in front of the king, saying how wonderful, smart, and wise he was. Then they would trick him into claiming he could read other people's minds and urge him to read their minds. In this way they would show he was a fraud.

The next day at court, they said to the king: "You're so lucky, Your Majesty. You have this wonderful, wise minister. He's so smart."

They said to the minister, "Aren't you smart?"

And the minister replied, "Yeah, I'm real smart."

Then they said: "You're so wise, you know everything. You probably even know what we're thinking."

"Yes, I know what you're thinking," he answered. He had fallen into the trap!

"OK, Minister, if you know what we're thinking, tell us in front of the king what it is." They had resolved that they would deny whatever he said just to put him in his place.

But then the minister said: "Yes, I know what you're thinking. You're all thinking kind thoughts toward His Majesty."

They had no choice but to say, "Yes, you're right."

They weren't thinking that at all, but if they had said otherwise, they would be in big trouble! Now that was someone who was really smart.

So when you, say, return home from a retreat and your husband asks you, "Did you learn anything on your retreat?" you should say, "Yes, darling, I learned how to read minds." When he asks you to read his mind, you can say, "You're thinking kind thoughts toward your wife, aren't you, darling?"

Some are born sprinters, while the majority of us are average runners. Although training will improve our results, we can only dream of running a hundred meters in ten seconds. There are also some among us who cannot run for a number of reasons. Is it similar with meditation?

No, because meditation uses wisdom power. When I was at school in London, we would do cross-country running in the winter. We would cross the River Thames on Hammersmith Bridge, go along the towpath to Barnes Bridge, cross again at Barnes Bridge, and then go back along the towpath to school.

The smart kids would bring along a few coins, and when they crossed Hammersmith Bridge, they would catch the bus to Barnes Bridge. The teacher would be on Barnes Bridge to make sure the kids actually got there. The kids would make sure they looked a bit sweaty, cross over, and then get the bus on the other side back to school. They were the smart kids.

So, yeah, some were born runners, but those who were smart would take the bus instead. If you use wisdom, you don't need to be a good sprinter to reach your destination.

Demons and Devas

Can a curse cause a spirit or a demon to possess someone who keeps the five precepts?

This is my personal experience with curses. While visiting England, I stayed with my mother in her apartment. One day she was making me lunch—lunch is very important for monks, because if we miss our lunch, that's it for the rest of the day—when somebody rang the doorbell. As my mother was in the middle of preparing lunch, I said, "Mother, I'll answer it." When I opened the door, it was a gypsy lady selling trinkets door to door.

I was very polite and said, "No, thank you—we don't need anything."

She said, "If you don't buy anything, I'll put a gypsy curse on you!"

She didn't know who she was playing with! So, standing there in my robes, I said: "I am a Buddhist monk. My curses are much stronger than yours!"

The poor woman turned around and ran away.

It was very funny, but maybe I went a bit too far. I scared the life out of her. Although it's true that monks can be powerful, we wouldn't curse anyone. But she didn't know that. Since Buddhist monks are still new to the West, people don't know if we will curse them or not. So I had fun with it.

But if you keep the five precepts, no one can curse you. Here's a classic story. At our monastery in Thailand, Wat Pah Nanachat, there was a young woman who would come every full moon day to stay at the temple. She kept the eight precepts once a week and the five precepts the rest of the time. She was a strong supporter who kept her precepts and was also a meditator.

One day she came to see us. That morning, when she looked in the bathroom mirror while washing her face, instead of seeing her own face, she saw the face of a monster! That freaked her out. She wasn't a crazy lady, and it was the first time she had seen something really weird.

And what do people in Thailand do in such a situation? They get the monks involved. So the next morning the monks went to her house to do a blessing ceremony and have lunch. While they were doing the ceremony, an old lady fainted. When she came to, she was speaking in a strange voice. The old Thai monk who was there, Ajahn Jun, knew what was going on. A spirit, a demon, had possessed this woman, not the young lady. The young lady was just looking on.

Ajahn Jun asked: "Who are you? What are you doing?" The spirit replied that he had been hired to kill the young woman by a spirit doctor in the nearby town of Ubon Ratchathani. A young man had wanted to go out with this girl and marry her, but she had turned him down. He was so upset that he had paid a spirit doctor to kill her.

The demon said he'd been trying to kill that girl for two years, but he hadn't been able to get even close to her. The monk said, "Look, you aren't going to be able to do anything to her because she's keeping her precepts very well and is living a very pure life."

The demon said: "If I don't kill her, I have to die myself. That's the deal."

The monk said, "It's better to die yourself than to kill someone else."

The demon actually accepted that, and the monk gave him the five precepts. Then the old woman fainted again, and she came out of her trance. Afterward she had no recollection of what had happened.

You probably haven't heard many such stories. Monks are sometimes privy to parts of life that are usually hidden. But the main message of that story is that possessions can happen, although they're rare. Further, if you keep the precepts, if you're morally pure, the demons can't get close to you. You're protected.

Here's another story. A girl in Perth brought her mother over from

Thailand because no one was looking after her there. One day her mother got sick, and she took her to King Edward Hospital in Perth. She went to a medium to find out if her mother was going to survive. For twenty bucks the medium would leave her body, go check on the mother, and then report back on her condition. All she needed was the mother's location.

After about ten minutes the medium came out of her trance. The first thing she did was return the girl's money.

"Why? What's going on?" the girl asked.

The medium said: "Well, I found the hospital, and I found the room, but I couldn't get inside. There was a force field around your mother, and I just couldn't penetrate it to find out whether she was going to survive or not." Then she asked: "Who is your mother? I've never seen anything like it before."

And that's when the girl said: "My mother is a Buddhist nun. She's been keeping the eight precepts for about thirty years."

At that, the medium took the twenty bucks back. "You should have told me beforehand. You've wasted my time. People like me can't get close to those sorts of people!"

This is the power of keeping precepts. From the point of view of a spirit or a ghost, you've got a force field around you. They can't get close to you or harm you. If you keep your precepts, you're safe. But if you break them—Wooooooh. . . .

So keep the precepts. Anyway, it's very rare for these things to harm you. Also, it's stupid to get spirits to harm someone else, because it always comes back to you.

You let go and you're healthy. But I know people who let go—who don't worry about diseases, who continue to smoke and drink—and their diseases don't go away. Can you explain why?

Smoking is always going to cause you problems, but worrying about it is not really a solution. I don't worry about diseases, but I'm not stupid, either. I rest. I look after my body.

If you're overweight, you have to laugh a lot. Father Christmas—ho, ho, ho—is fat, healthy, and never dies! That's my trick to compensate for being overweight. Last year I read an article about how laughing and being happy expands your blood vessels. Because I laugh a lot, my blood vessels are like super highways. They are so wide that there are no traffic jams: they don't get clogged up with all the grease and other stuff in my system. So the more you laugh, the fatter you can be and still be healthy. This also explains why fat people are jolly—it's because all the miserable fat ones died a long time ago! So if you're a little overweight, laugh, quickly—it might save your life! Actually, there's a lot of truth in that. Let go and don't worry, because worry is the biggest killer. Even if you've got some sort of disease, fear kills you more than anything else. This is the theme of Edgar Allen Poe's "The Mask of the Red Death," in which a number of devils go to the major cities of Europe to cause a plague. Afterward they meet somewhere in the forest to compare notes. The dialogue goes something like this:

"How many people did you kill in London?"

"Oh, I killed a hundred people in London."

"How many people did you kill in Paris?"

"Oh, I killed a hundred and fifty in Paris."

"How many in Berlin?"

"Oh, I only killed fifty in Berlin, and fear killed four thousand." (Or something like that!)

I thought, "What a great insight that fear kills more people than any disease." So, fear is the one thing that you should really be afraid of. In other words, don't be afraid at all. Worry is more likely to kill you than anything else. Please don't worry. But do look after your health; don't do stupid things.

> It's amazing what useless things people ask heavenly beings for help with—lottery tickets, lost car keys. No wonder they get annoyed and don't come down much! If it's a question about the meaning of life or how to meditate better, then perhaps they'll help. So ask them for help only if it's really important.

So King Rama was a deva, a heavenly being. Presumably he had made much good kamma in his human life to be reborn as a deva. But aren't devas immortal? How do they escape the cycle of samsara if they're immortal?

Devas are not immortal. They're just in the deva realm for a while, and when that kamma is used up, they get reborn elsewhere. It's just like going on a holiday: when you run out of cash, you have to go back home and get to work again. In the same way, you have a nice time in the deva realms because you've made lots of good kamma. But when you run out of good kamma, you have to come back and make more.

The Lord Buddha described life in other worlds. Do you believe in devas? If so, where do they live? Can we see devas when we meditate?

Yes, there are supposed to be other worlds—just because you haven't seen them doesn't mean they don't exist. Here's the best deva story I know. I can confirm that it's a real deva story, because I know the guy who was involved.

A young American was doing Peace Corps work in Thailand. After two years he decided to become a monk. He'd come to understand Thai culture and respect Buddhism. He thought: "What a good idea! Before I go back to the US and get my career going, I'll become a monk for a short time."

He was staying in a hotel on the outskirts of Bangkok and asked the concierge what he should do. The concierge knew a lot of places to go in Bangkok, but not a lot of monasteries. He did, however, know one monastery in the middle of the city called Wat Bovorn, where there were sometimes Western monks. He told the American to go to Wat Bovorn early in the morning, to take some food to offer to the monks on almsround, and then to tell them he wanted to ordain.

He was so eager that he left very early the next morning, only to arrive at Wat Bovorn when the monastery was still locked. Wondering what to do, he just walked up and down. A Thai man came up to him and asked him what he was doing. He told him that he had come to offer some food and that he wanted to become a monk, but the place was locked.

The Thai man said it was far too early. The monks wouldn't be out until dawn, which was another couple of hours away. But he said it didn't matter, because he had the key. He would let him in and show him around. He got out a bunch of keys, opened the old metal gate, and took him inside the main ordination hall where all the ceremonies were performed.

The Thai man opened the door to the main hall and turned on the lights. In the temples in Bangkok there are murals on the walls. The murals tell a story. You have to find out where to start, and then you follow the pictures in the right sequence, like a comic strip. Sometimes it weaves all over the place. If you know the story, you can work out the characters and see how the plot unfolds.

The Thai man knew everything about the paintings, including who sponsored them and why. Some people did it because they wanted to make merit for a dead child, for example. The man was so well informed that the American was fascinated. Then, with perfect timing, just as they got to the last painting, the man said: "The monks are coming in about five minutes. Go out there, stand at the front, and wait for an old monk to come out. Maybe some young monks will come first, but wait for the old one. When he comes out, put some food in his bowl, and ask him for ordination." The Thai man locked up and turned off the lights.

The American did as the Thai man said. When the old monk came out, the American put some food in the monk's bowl, and said, "I want to become a monk."

"Wait here until I come back, and I'll take you inside," the old monk replied. That was how the American got started in his monastic training.

A few days later a monk was appointed to teach him the chanting and the basic monastic rules, but his English was poor. The American got a bit frustrated, and one day he said, "Isn't there anyone who speaks better English?"

The monks replied, "No, this is the best person we have."

"What about the temple attendant who let me in on the first day? He spoke perfect English."

Intrigued, they asked, "What temple attendant?"

"The one who opened the gate and showed me inside," he said.

At that, they took him straight to the abbot. You see, there was no temple attendant who spoke perfect English! The American told the abbot about what had happened on the first morning when he arrived. The abbot got the monastery secretary to write everything down from the very beginning.

They took the story so seriously not only because there was no temple attendant who spoke perfect English, but also because the American had entered the temple through the royal gate. Wat Bovorn is actually a royal temple; it's where the kings of Thailand ordain as monks for short periods of time. And the only people allowed through the royal gate were royalty. Not even the head monk could use that gate. Furthermore, only the abbot and his attendant had a key.

Also, there was no light switch at the place where "the attendant" had turned on the lights. And no layperson had the key to the hall. In addition, not even the old abbot knew all that much about the paintings. So much about what had happened was weird. When the American finished telling his story, the abbot, who later became the Sangharaja of Thailand, asked: "What did he look like? Can you remember his features?"

Just at that moment, the American glanced up, and saw a portrait on the wall.

"It was him!" he said excitedly. "That's who it was!"

It was King Rama IV, a former king of Thailand! That's why he could walk through the royal gate. And the reason he knew all about those paintings was that he had been there when they were done, about 150 years before.

I know that monk. That's a true story of a deva, of an old Thai king reborn as a deva who came down to help a Westerner become a monk. Devas do exist.

In the suttas, there are descriptions of different planes of existence, from various heavenly planes to the hell realm. In the Tāvatiṁsa world, there are fights within and between deva planes. If deva realms are places of enjoyment, why are there fights? Then there's the deva Sakka, who has huge merit and hundreds of wives. And is this really a place of pleasure for the devis if many are married to the same deva? In hell, there are hell wardens, physical torture, people reading out a person's wrongdoings before they're punished, and so on. I thought all this was myth, but it seems real and literal in the suttas. Is it because my colored mind cannot understand what's beyond me that it seems mythical? I hope this is not too shallow a question.

It's not too shallow a question. Thank you for asking it, because these sorts of things have bothered me as a rational Buddhist, one who believes in science. I could understand the high heavenly realms—that made the most sense to me—but some of these lower realms? Not so much.

You may not be able to understand these realms until you really get into your meditation and realize the power of the mind. When you get into the realm of the nimittas, where the body starts to disappear and you get mental images, you'll see that the range of mental images is huge. But most of what you experience has been added by your perception—the colors of nimittas, the shapes, or whatever. You realize just how much of this world you create with the mind.

From that I realized that the hell realms are self-created. If you've done some bad kamma and you're headed for hell, it's only because you think you deserve to go there. That's all. No one sends you there; you send yourself. No one reads out your past misdeeds—you remember them and then judge yourself. You stay down there as long as you feel you deserve it. It's called guilt. It's very helpful to understand the power of guilt and how it's released through forgiveness, through letting go of the past. Even in this life, many of you have done bad things. Because of that you feel guilty, and you actually punish yourself in this life. If you still remember it at the end of your life, you'll punish yourself again. All you need to do is let that past go. You don't need to feel guilty. You can forgive.

This is what one does in meditation. How do you learn to forgive? You learn how to lose the "me" identification, the sense of "self," the identification with past deeds. When you see nonself deeply, you fully let go of the idea of "me" and you become a stream-winner. You cannot be reborn in the lower realms anymore, including the animal realm, no matter what you've done. Why? Once you become a stream-winner, once you see the nature of what you've taken to be "yourself," forgiveness becomes so easy. Because you know there's no self, it's easy to forgive and let go. When you're able to let go and forgive—both what you have done to others and what others have done to you—you feel so free. You realize that you don't have to feel bad about the past.

When you go to the heaven realms, you make them to suit you. We've got two Norwegian monks at our monastery, and they told me about Valhalla. Valhalla (the hall of the slain) was where "good" Vikings would go—it's their heaven realm. You only go there after you've died in battle, as a "good" Viking. Valhalla is a big hall where there's a big feast with lots of alcohol. You eat and you drink and then you have a fight. You all kill each other, and then you wake up again with more eating, more drinking, and more fighting. The reason the heaven realm was like that is that that's what the Vikings loved. Eating, drinking, and fighting most of all—that was their idea of heaven. No girls! Just the real "blokey" stuff. Whatever you like, whatever you think of as heaven, that's what you get.

People from Singapore have a Singapore heaven created just by them: it's got the best coffee shops and restaurants, open twenty-four hours a day, and they can keep on eating and eating and eating and eating without ever getting full. In the Singaporean heaven realm, the stock market always goes up, up, up, up, and up, never down.

So the reason some heavenly beings fight is that they enjoy fighting. It's mind-made, like fantasy, like virtual reality. The mind makes a heaven realm to suit you. That's why in some of these realms you can have a hundred wives, if that's what you enjoy. They aren't real wives; they're just created by you.

The realms the Buddha described were the most common ones in those days. There are other realms mentioned in the suttas, such as that of the *khiḍḍāpadosika* devas (DN 1). These are the devas who love playing. They just mess around all the time, tell jokes, and play practical tricks on each other, because that's what they enjoy.

Whatever heaven realm you like, that's the one you go to. You make it. You think you deserve it, and you stay there as long as that's the case. When you think you've had enough, you go on to another rebirth.

If you have guilt, you feel that you have to pay for your past misdeeds, that you have to be punished, then you create a hell realm for yourself. The realms you see in the murals of old temples are examples of how these things get created. These days we have totally different ideas of hell. I remember being in Penang, teaching a retreat one Christmas. On Christmas Day, after the evening questions-and-answers session, around 10:30 p.m., I went to have a rest. But on the opposite side of the road there was a party going on. I don't mind parties, but this was a karaoke party! Now, *that* is suffering!

For me, hell would be a karaoke bar that never closed! So the heavens and hells are what we create.

Better than Sex?

If you let it be and don't focus on it, can meditation make sex more meaningful, sensuous, and fun?

It's in the precepts that you're not supposed to have sex when you're on retreat. You're supposed to let go of the body, not indulge in the body. And you don't let it *be*, you let it *go*. You focus on the breath; you focus on the nimittas. It's much better than sex. Actually, sex will destroy your meditation.

This is one of the things that got me into being a monk. If you know the joy of meditation, the question of sex never comes up. Who wants to masturbate or have sex when you can sit down quietly on a cushion and get a bliss that is far better?!

A year ago someone took me to task for talking about "the bliss better than sex." He said the bliss of jhāna is in a different league; it doesn't even bear comparison. I apologized, because the bliss of jhāna is way beyond, way superior, and the two shouldn't even be compared. Get into deep meditation and know that for yourself.

> Anyone can get jhāna. I'm not saying you will, but you can. There's nothing preventing you. It's wisdom that does it, not willpower. Being smart is how you achieve it.

Should we focus on the meditation object or on the lights? Our ultimate goal is one-pointedness and to let our body vanish. Is this the important thing, or is it the lights?

The lights are just what happens when you make peace and are mindful and kind. If you try to focus on them they disappear. Don't think, "I am now going to focus on the lights" or, "I am now going to get one-pointedness." The only thing you should focus on—if you're focusing on anything at all—is mindfulness and kindness, "kindfulness." If you do that, everything happens by itself.

The jhāna factors—*vitakka*, *vicāra*, *pīti*, *sukha*, and *ekaggatā*—most people haven't got a clue what they are. So get into a jhāna first of all, and then when you come out afterward you'll understand. The jhāna factors are not different things; they're five aspects of the same experience. They *are* the first jhāna.

One-pointedness is not really a good term. The word *agga*, in *ekaggatā*, means "a peak or a capital," like *Agra* in Sanskrit, which was the capital of the Mughal Empire in India. *Aggatā* refers to the summit of the mind, not "pointedness." *Aggatā* means "a really unified state of mind," with bliss as your only focus. You should stay with that bliss for minute after minute, hour after hour. *Ekaggatā* means "singleness of mind" and also "singleness through time."

Why did the Buddha teach that extreme forms of pleasure and pain are to be avoided, and yet jhāna is a pleasure greater than sex?

The Buddha only said that the pleasures of the five senses are to be avoided, not all pleasures, like jhāna. The five types of sense pleasure are distractions, and they stop you from developing the pleasure of the mind. This teaching is in the *Araṇavibhaṅga Sutta* (MN 139), which says that we need to distinguish between the pleasures of the five senses and the pleasures of the mind.

The pleasures of the mind, the Buddha said, should be cultivated, including inspiration. If you hear a teaching that really goes to your heart, you should develop the pleasure of inspiration. If you see someone being compassionate and kind, indulge in the happiness of seeing a compassionate act. Indulge in the happiness of your own mind. Those are the pleasures we're supposed to indulge in.

Sense pleasures are one extreme, but we are supposed to avoid the other extreme of pain too—like listening to my jokes for too long!

The suttas say that the Buddha, upon attaining the fourth jhāna, directed his mind to the destruction of the taints. How does one do this after jhāna?

There are three taints, or outflowings: *kāmāsava*, *avijjāsava*, and *bhavāsava*. *Āsava* is often translated as "taint," but I prefer "outflowing."

The first one, *kāmāsava*, is looking for happiness in the world of the five senses. That's destroyed when you realize what true happiness really is. When you come out of jhāna, you've just had the greatest bliss of your life, way beyond any pleasures of the five senses. You realize that true happiness comes from letting go of the five senses, from letting them disappear. As a consequence, you lose interest in seeking happiness in the world of the five senses and sense desire comes to an end. This is the destruction of the kāmāsava.

The more interesting one is the *avijjāsava*. *Avijjā* is illusion. Illusion, as the Buddha said, is thinking that what is suffering is happiness and what is happiness is suffering, getting it all the wrong way round (AN 4:49). Have you noticed that when a baby is born the family is happy but the baby cries? They're not paying any attention to how the baby feels. And when someone dies, the corpse is smiling but everyone else is crying? They get it the wrong way round!

We should really take our cues from the person experiencing these things. When a baby is born, cry: "Ooooh, how sad it is! Ooooh, I've got another kid to look after, to keep me awake at night. Ooooh, I've got another grandchild to worry about." Do all you grandparents cry when you find out your daughter has given birth? Do you say, "Oh, that's so sad"? When someone tells me, "My daughter has just given birth to a son," I say, "My condolences." They think I'm crazy.

When someone dies, I go: "Woo-hooo! Marvelous! When's the party?" Especially if someone dies young. If you die young, you don't have to go to an old people's home!

You should be like the Ven. Dr. K. Sri Dhammananda. When his oncologist told him that his cancer was terminal and that there was nothing that could be done for him, he burst out laughing. The oncologist said that Venerable Dhammananda was the only guy he'd ever known who had burst out laughing when he was told he was terminally ill. That's because he was a monk, someone who really understood Buddhism. So when they say you're going to die, you should laugh: "Hahahahaha! *Sādhu*!"

The third āsava, *bhavāsava*, is the outflowing of existence. The āsava of existence is destroyed when we realize there's no one in here. In deep meditation, especially in the jhānas, you actually see that there's no one home. You look in the body and you look in the mind, and you can't find Ajahn Brahm anywhere; you can't find anyone anywhere. When you know there's no one there, it has a profound effect. The sense of self no longer drives you to do things. You can be totally lazy and people can call you a pig. But *who's* a pig?

You know the three characteristics of existence, right? *Anicca*, *dukkha*, and *anattā*? *Anicca* is "impermanence," *dukkha* "suffering," and *anattā* "nonself." Anicca, Dukkha, and Anattā walk into a bar.

Dukkha says, "This bar sucks."

Anicca says, "Don't worry, it'll change."

And Anattā says, "Who said that?"

When you realize that there's no one home, that's when the outflowing of existence vanishes; that's what happens after jhāna. That's how the āsavas are destroyed.

Laypeople can get into jhāna, become stream-winners, and become enlightened just like monastics. So, if I'm serious about being on this path, is there really any advantage in being a monastic rather than a layperson?

The difference between monks and nuns and you is that we have renounced much more, let go of much more. We've let go of sex and our family, including the people we'd normally care the most about, such as husbands or wives.

There's an amazing case of a lady in Perth who really dominated her husband. When they came to the monastery to offer *dāna* (charity), she would say to him in public, "George, you stupid man, come over here and do this; go over there and do that." I felt really sorry for George. Then she died. I thought he would be so happy, but instead he said, "I miss her so much!" I thought this was crazy—she'd given him such a hard time. But he had got used to it and loved it! I thought he would feel as if he'd been freed from jail, but instead he was pining. That's how attached one gets.

Try being a monk or a nun. It'll show you how much monks and nuns renounce. It isn't the same kind of practice. A layperson like you can renounce—take the eight precepts—by spending nine days on retreat at our monastery. But then you go back home, watch movies, catch up on sports, and eat whatever you want whenever you want it. It's very different and much more difficult to renounce fully for the rest of your life. That's why the amount of letting go for monastics is much greater. That's why there are monastics, why the Buddha set up the Sangha. It's a faster, more thorough path of letting go. We don't have any money. We don't follow any fashion. We just wear our brown robes, and that's it. It's a much simpler life.

Bogus Buddhas?

Is it true that there were many buddhas before Sakyamuni? Will there be any buddhas after him? If yes, will all the buddhas be teaching the same thing? What's the difference between a buddha and an arahant?

This is all about cause and effect, not about people. The Dhamma and the eightfold path are always there, waiting to be discovered. When the current teaching disappears, sooner or later someone will become enlightened again. If he starts teaching, that person is called a buddha. So a buddha is just the person who starts the teaching going again, and all those who become enlightened by following that teaching are called arahants. The Buddha is number one, the first in the lineage. Eventually his teachings die out, and then another buddha arises.

What about our Buddha? Where did he come from? Did he discover everything by himself? That's what traditional Buddhists say, but it isn't supported by the evidence. There's an interesting sutta, the *Ghaṭīkāra Sutta*, in the Majjhima Nikāya (MN 81), in which our buddha, Buddha Gotama, remembered a past life during the time of the previous buddha, Buddha Kassapa.

Kassapa had a chief disciple called Ghaṭīkāra, a poor potter, who was a nonreturner. The only reason he didn't become a monk was that he had to look after his mother and father, who were both blind.

Although he was a potter, he was so virtuous that to avoid hurting living beings he never dug the earth. To make his pots he took the clay left over by farmers who had been repairing the dykes in their paddy fields, or the clay dug up by rabbits or rats. He wouldn't even risk harming a worm! And he didn't sell his pots for money. Instead, he put them on a bench outside his shop with a sign: "If anyone wants a pot, please take one. If anyone wants to leave some rice and beans, please do so. I've got to look after my parents." So there was no selling, either.

You can see that he was just totally nonmaterialistic and very kind, and he did his work just to look after his parents. And of course people knew that, so they wouldn't take a pot without leaving something for him. No buying and selling, just donation, the way we do it in our monastery.

Ghaṭīkāra had a friend called Jotipāla, who was not interested in religion. When Ghaṭīkāra said, "Come and see the Buddha Kassapa—he's very wise and compassionate," Jotipāla said: "Who wants to see that shaven-headed idiot? You guys and your religion!"

He wasn't into that at all. But eventually Ghaṭīkāra tricked his friend into seeing the Buddha Kassapa. Jotipāla was so impressed that he went for refuge and ordained as a *bhikkhu* (a monk).

When Buddha Gotama told this story, he revealed that he had been Jotipāla under the previous buddha. You would think that someone with that degree of good kamma—learning under a buddha—would at least become a stream-winner, or even a once-returner. It is said that when the Buddha was born he took seven steps and said, "This is my last birth" (MN 123). How would he have known that unless he was a once-returner? It is also said that once-returners get reborn in the Tusita realm, which is where the Buddha came from. This is circumstantial but strong evidence indicating that Buddha Gotama had been a once-returner who then became enlightened in this life and was the first one to do so in this Buddha-cycle. That's why he was called the Buddha. According to the *Ghaṭīkāra Sutta* (SN 1:50), one of the devas who came down to congratulate the Buddha after his enlightenment was Ghaṭīkāra, who had been reborn in the nonreturner realm. He said, "We were friends together in the same village. We went to see Buddha Kassapa together. I'm still an anāgāmī, and you're a Buddha. Congratulations!" Or something to that effect.

Brahmā Sahampati, the deva who invited the Buddha to teach (MN 26), was also a monk under Buddha Kassapa. They were all friends and disciples of Buddha Kassapa. Two of them, Ghaṭīkāra and Sahampati, became anāgāmīs and were reborn in the pure abodes. Sahampati also came down to congratulate his friend Jotipāla, now Gotama, our Buddha.

So you see, there are many buddhas. Just before Buddha Gotama became enlightened, he used the power of his meditation to remember his past lives (MN 36). He would certainly have remembered his past life under Buddha Kassapa, and he would probably have recalled being taught the four noble truths. So did he discover the four noble truths? Or did he remember them? I will let you think about that.

There's a book called the *Anāgatavaṁsa*, which gives the names of ten future buddhas. Where did those names come from?

They were made up. They didn't come from the Buddha; they came later. The only future buddha mentioned in the suttas is Metteyya, but even he is mentioned only once, and it doesn't seem likely to have really been the word of the Buddha.

So where did this book come from? And what was the purpose of writing it?

The city of Medan, in Indonesia, has the biggest Buddhist temple in Southeast Asia, and it's dedicated to Metteyya. It was mainly built by a Taiwanese group whose thinking was that there's no Buddhism left and so it's best to worship Metteyya and earn enough good kamma to be reborn when he's around.

But that's absolutely ridiculous! The teachings of the Buddha are alive and well. And Buddha Gotama is still here in the sense that the Dhamma is here. This is a major problem: People want to know about the future rather than worry about the present. It's a terrible thing that really destroys Buddhism. When everyone's waiting for Metteyya to come, everyone's waiting for the future, rather than being in the present and getting enlightened now.

So that's where that sort of book comes from. You can get much more money for your temple by encouraging people to pray to someone who's not here rather than to meditate, because meditation is much harder work!

> You don't choose a religious path; it chooses you. You listen to the teachings of Buddhism or whatever religion, and after a while you think, "Hey, this is me!" That's certainly what happened to me. I was reading about different religions, and when I read a book on Buddhism, I realized that I already was a Buddhist! I just hadn't known it. If you are seeking, it will find you.

7.

Dhamma and Greg

Wrapping it up for the Buddha-heads.

Of the eight worldly winds, power and fame are the opposite of powerlessness. Is powerlessness not knowing what's going on in life, and is it associated with vulnerability?

The eight worldly winds (*loka-dhamma*) are praise and blame, fame and notoriety, happiness and suffering, and gain and loss. The winds of power and fame are the opposite of powerlessness, but you don't necessarily get powerful because you're famous. In fact, the more famous you are, the less possibility there is for you to do what you want.

A long time ago, Angie, who was then the president of the Buddhist Fellowship in Singapore, said to me: "You'd better be careful, Ajahn Brahm. So many people in Singapore know you. If you do anything wrong or mischievous, I'll know!"

I thought, "My goodness—I'd better behave!"

We had a vote about whether we should wear cold weather jackets or not at Bodhinyana Monastery or whether we should just do whatever we want. I said, "Either everyone should wear a jacket or no one should." But I was outvoted. Now the monks wear jackets whenever they want. I've got no power.

The reality is that you don't have any power to begin with. You're not in control. I sometimes illustrate this with the simile of the driverless bus.

Life is like a journey on a bus. Sometimes you travel through very beautiful scenery: wonderful alpine mountains, beautiful waterfalls, and rolling meadows with cows serenely grazing. It's so wonderful that you want to say: "Stop! I wanna take a photo. I wanna enjoy this wonderful scenery." You try to tell the bus driver—the one in charge of your life—to slow down so you can enjoy it all for as long as possible. But the bus driver puts his foot on the accelerator and speeds away.

At another time, you're passing through one of the toxic-waste dumps of life, a degraded industrial area with graffiti on the walls and syringes on the sidewalk. You try to tell the bus driver: "Ah! This is dangerous and scary and ugly. Get out of here as soon as you can." But the bus driver brakes and stops. That's life.

When things go wrong in life, we sometimes ask: "Why do they go wrong? Why can't I get out of here more quickly? Why does my stupid bus driver brake when it's all so unpleasant, painful, and disappointing? Why does the suffering last so long?"

And when there's happiness, we ask: "Why doesn't it last longer? Why can't I stop to enjoy the happy moments of life?" It's because the bus driver is stupid! That's why!

The bus driver's name is Will.

Because you think the only way to have a happy life is to go quickly through the painful times and to slow down to enjoy the pleasant ones, you decide to teach Will how to drive. But in order to teach Will how to drive, how to be wise, you've first got to find him. That's the job of meditation, of stillness and insight.

In meditation you finally go deep inside and you find the bus driver's seat, Will's seat, the place where all these choices are made. That's when you get the shock of your life—the seat is empty! There's no one sitting behind the wheel! The bus driver of your life doesn't exist! It's all causes and conditions, a process. No one's driving; no one is in charge. You're out of control.

As a result of that realization, you go back to your seat and stop complaining. The reason you stop complaining is that there's no one to complain to! Suffering or happiness is just part of life.

No craving, no ill will, no complaining anymore. The end of the illusion of an autonomous will means the end of craving. You know there's no bus driver and that you have no power.

Has trying to be in control gotten you anywhere? You've gotten nowhere. That's par for the course. So just enjoy it. Let go. No control. You're being vulnerable, but vulnerable to peace and wisdom. That's marvelous.

We don't like being peaceful because we're afraid. We don't like being wise because we don't know what it might mean for us. We'd rather stay in our comfort zone, where everything is familiar, just like people in prison. When they're told their release date is coming up, they don't want to leave. They're comfortable in prison; it's familiar. They'd rather stay there than have freedom—just like us.

There's a wonderful story in my book *Opening the Door of Your Heart* about a worm and its lovely pile of dung.

There were once two monks. They were the best of friends and they hung out together their whole lives. When they died, one of them, who was a very good monk, was reborn in a heavenly realm, while the other one, because he was too lazy and slept too much, was reborn as a worm in a pile of dung.

The heavenly being was wondering where his friend had been reborn. He looked for his friend in all the heavenly realms but couldn't find him anywhere. "Ah," he thoughts, "he must have been reborn as a human being, because that too is a good rebirth."

Using his heavenly psychic powers, he searched the entire human realm, but couldn't find him anywhere. "Oh my goodness!" he thought. "Perhaps he has been reborn as an animal." He checked all the big animals—such as the elephants and the tigers—but couldn't find him among them either.

Then he checked out the creepy crawlies, and to his disgust and horror found his friend there. Although he had been a monk in his previous life, he had been reborn as a worm in a pile of cow dung. The heavenly being thought, "I can't just leave my friend in such a terrible condition."

He went down to the pile of cow dung and called out to his friend. The little worm poked his head out of the pile and said, "What do you want?"

"We were best friends in our previous life. We were monks together. Now, because of my good kamma, I've been reborn in heaven.

It's beautiful up there. It's unfortunate that you were reborn in this pile of dung, but I can help you. Come on. Come up to heaven with me. I'll take you."

"Hang on a moment! Is there any dung in heaven?"

"Of course not. Dung is disgusting."

"Then I'm not going. I like my dung. I eat it, and it's delicious! It's where I live, and it's nice and warm. It's fragrant. If there's no dung in heaven, can I take some with me?"

"No!"

"Then I don't wanna go."

The heavenly being thought: "If only I could show him heaven, he could experience it for himself. I'm sure he'd like it, and he'd understand with insight that heaven is much better than a pile of dung."

He grabbed the worm and tried to pull him out of the dung. But because the worm was covered with slimy dung, he was able to wriggle away and escape to the deepest part of the dung pile. Owing to their deep friendship, the heavenly being held his nose and put his hand deep into the dung. Eventually he found his friend and again tried to pull him out. The worm complained, shouted, wriggled, and soon escaped his grasp.

Every time the heavenly being almost got his worm-friend out, his friend got away. After many, many tries, the heavenly being had to go back to Bodhinyana Monastery, and all the little worms had to go back to their homes and jobs.

Why is it like this? Because, "I like my dung—it's my home and it's fragrant."

Why won't you let go of your dung? It's fascinating, isn't it? It's called attachment. If you get into jhāna a few times—"Wow!" you'll think, "this is better than sex"—you'll know what true happiness is. You'll understand what's dung and what's heaven. It will change you.

Attachments and Other Discontents

What is the fuel for discontent? What is the fuel for contentment?

The fuel for discontent is thinking that happiness lies somewhere else, that enlightenment is somewhere other than where you are already. We say that discontent or suffering is the distance between where you want to be and where you are. Where do you want to be? Is that where you are? If it's not, that's called discontent.

How do you solve the problem? Try changing your idea of where you want to be, making it where you are: "I don't want to be anywhere, except right here, in this seat, with my stupid, restless, dull mind, which is all over the place. I just want to be here." Then there's no discontent. If you're content, fully content, you'll be surprised that restlessness and sloth and torpor just vanish.

Being content with where you are is the meaning of making peace. Be here without wanting to be somewhere else, because that's being dishonest to your reality. Just be here. Then all your craving, your wanting, your striving—all the stuff that keeps agitating your mind—just disappears. "I'm satisfied with being dull, I'm satisfied with being restless"—when you make peace with all that, you're letting go of craving, you're following the path of the Buddha, and soon you'll be enlightened. Stop creating this distance, this separation, between where you are and where you want to be.

Can you please explain letting go of attachments and likes and dislikes?

Attachment is what's between you and what you think you own. It's an aspect of your sense of self. Letting go of attachments means you don't always have the same likes and dislikes. Attachment is optional, but we all have likes and dislikes, even the Buddha had them.

Once the Buddha was confronted by a monster called Sūciloma, whose name translates as "Needle-hair." He was a prototype punk with needles for hair! He wanted to find out if the Buddha was really enlightened. So he sat down next to the Buddha and leaned toward him to prick him, but the Buddha leaned away.

"Aha!" said Needle-Hair. "You don't like pain. You're not really enlightened. An enlightened person would maintain equanimity no matter what. He wouldn't have any likes or dislikes."

The Buddha said: "Don't be stupid. There are things that are going to cause problems for my body. It's going to hurt it and make it unhealthy" (SN 10:53).

This is just common sense. You don't step on snakes, you don't run into fires, and you don't allow needles to poke you. You move away. It's common sense, not attachment. That's loving-kindness toward your body: keeping it healthy, keeping it safe.

A lot of the time likes and dislikes are just loving-kindness. I like the Buddhist Society of Western Australia. I like serving and teaching. Is that attachment? No. It's just that there are things you like and things you don't like. I like fish and chips: it's my conditioning—my hormones, my body, and everything else. I can't help it; it's the way I was brought up. That's not attachment.

Likes and dislikes are different from attachment. Attachment is the sense of self grabbing on to something.

Why is it so difficult to let go of attachments, even though they cause suffering?

It's because we'd rather be in pain than not exist and be happy. Of the three types of craving (craving for sensual pleasure, craving for existence, and craving for nonexistence), the craving to exist is more basic than the craving to be happy. That's why people who are dying often won't let go of the body, even though they are really uncomfortable. They won't let go because they fear annihilation more than they fear pain. The craving to exist is the fundamental, the most important, attachment. We would rather be in pain than not exist at all.

Please elaborate on the concepts of gratification, danger, and escape. Why do we have to have gratification—why not just danger and escape?

These just refer to things that go on in our minds. Take thinking. Why do people think? Because of the gratification. There's a delight in thinking. Why do you get angry? Because there's a delight in getting angry. Think of people who've hurt you: "Those stupid people, they shouldn't have done that!" It makes you feel alive! So there's a joy in getting angry.

I don't have to say anything about the gratification of lust—everyone knows about that. And of course there's gratification in such things as sleeping and eating.

But there's also gratification in negative mind states. If there were no gratification in jealousy and other negative emotions, we wouldn't have them. We have them because there's a joy in them.

But there's also a danger in them. Yeah, it's good fun to get angry and shout at someone—because they really need to be told off and you feel good afterward—but then comes the danger when they tell you off in return, and you get into big trouble. Lust? Wow, it's really good fun, until you have babies, or until you get into trouble with your partner because you have lust for somebody else.

And, you know, fantasizing and dreaming seem like such good ideas. You don't have any pain in your meditation, you don't have to worry about your breath, and you can plan and dream about all sorts of things. But there's a danger there afterward. You get tired and you think, "I'm wasting my time!"

When you see the danger in things, you realize, "Yeah, there's joy in this, but there's also danger, and the danger outweighs the joy." It's like drinking alcohol. People enjoy it, but there's a danger: you have to pay for it with a hangover. There's gratification in gambling. You almost win, and you think, "This is great fun." But you might end up losing a lot of money. You know the gratification of shopping, and then you know the danger when you get the credit card bill at the end of the month.

When you know there's gratification and you know there's danger, you're being honest. You can ask, "Does the danger outweigh the gratification?" When you understand that it does, you say no to these things. Once you understand the danger, you understand that it's not worthwhile.

What's the escape from these things? It's much the same thing: seeing the gratification and the danger with wisdom; seeing what's really going on in life. You then have a greater sense of control over your life, in a good sense. You don't want to go down a path that leads to danger, and you get the freedom just by noticing this. The knowing is the escape. "What am I doing that for?" It doesn't make any sense anymore. That's the moral of the following story.

Even as a student I gave up drinking alcohol. In the early days I would sometimes get drunk because no one told me to do otherwise. There was pleasure—being with your friends and having a good time. But the danger became clear the following morning. I was wise enough to think: "What am I doing this for? Alcohol is expensive! It doesn't really do anything for me. You lose all your mindfulness. You can't remember much of what happened the previous evening." So I gave it up. Giving it up, you get so many health benefits as well.

I thought I was really making a big sacrifice. I thought I'd never get invited to any parties. In Australia they have a word for a person like that, a *wowser.* A wowser is someone who doesn't enjoy a party, someone who doesn't drink. Wowsers don't get into all the mischief other people do. They're party poopers. But instead of not getting invited, I was invited to even more parties! Why? Because they wanted someone sober to drive them home!

That was me. Being sober, I actually got more party invites. People trusted me more, and that was another benefit.

I saw the benefits of alcohol and I saw the dangers. When I saw that the dangers outweighed the benefits, I gave it up. It was as simple as that. Wisdom was the escape.

Use the same method in your meditation. See the danger of thinking. Where does it get you? It just gives you headaches. You never get wise through thinking. When you see the danger of thinking, you're not interested anymore. You let it go. That's the escape.

> If you want more, you can't enjoy what you already have—that's the essence of Buddhism. Even if you're a billionaire—with yachts and private jets, with big mansions and butlers—if you want more, you can't enjoy whatever you already have. But even if you're a poor person, even just a monk or a nun, if you don't want anything, even in meditation, you can enjoy everything.

THE BUDDHA SAID THE DARNEDEST THINGS

Please explain the sublime abidings.

The term *sublime abidings* usually refers to the four *brahmavihāras*: *mettā*, *karuṇā*, *muditā*, and *upekkhā*. *Mettā* (loving-kindness) is, "May all beings be happy and well." *Karuṇā* (compassion) is, "May all beings be free from suffering." *Muditā* (joy) is rejoicing with beings who are happy; it's the beautiful selfless joy in other people's happiness. If the meditator next to you has just become enlightened, you think, "Oh, I am so glad for you that you're enlightened." It's the opposite of: "It's really unfair! It's her first meditation retreat and she's got it already! I've been to ten, and I'm not enlightened yet! This sucks!" And *upekkhā* (equanimity) is an attitude of calmness and stillness, a looking on with deep peace.

They're called *sublime abidings* when they're the cause for deep meditation. Mettā, as has been much discussed, is a beautiful way of meditating. You think, "May all beings be happy and well," and you feel the sensation afterward until the mettā gets very strong. If you want to, you can do mettā with your breath: "May my in-breaths be happy and well. I really care for you in-breath; just go in with my blessing. Out-breath, have a great time as you go out. May all my outbreaths be happy and well. May all my in-breaths be free from pain." When you do mettā toward your breath, your breath becomes soft, gentle, beautiful, and peaceful, and it's very easy to meditate.

You can apply all of these, although it can be difficult to do karuṇā because of the focus on suffering and pain. I don't normally recommend it, because it can bring you down when you focus on the suffering in life. But muditā is good, and so is upekkhā. Focus on the positive side. This gives you a beautiful, sublime abiding of peace.

Can you talk more about the third noble truth of letting go in relation to the second noble truth of clinging?

I teach meditation by distinguishing between second-noble-truth meditation and third-noble-truth meditation. This is important to understand. For those of you who don't know your Buddhism, the second noble truth says that craving leads to suffering, and the third noble truth says that letting go of craving leads to the end of suffering—happiness, peace, nibbāna.

What is second-noble-truth meditation? "I want. I want. I want."

The Buddha said that leads to suffering. So if you're frustrated, if you're disappointed, if the meditation isn't peaceful, you've just been doing second-noble-truth meditation—you've been wanting something. Please don't do second-noble-truth meditation. On the other hand, if you're getting peaceful, well done! You're practicing third-noble-truth meditation—letting go of wanting—and you're headed toward peace and nibbāna.

It's very clear that too many people do second-noble-truth meditation: "I want jhāna." "I want a nimitta." "I want psychic powers." You'll just suffer, because you're creating the cause of suffering.

Instead, do third-noble-truth meditation: let go, let go, let go; make peace, be kind, be gentle. That leads to freedom, to peace, to nibbāna. Trust the Buddha's teachings. The Buddha knew what he was talking about.

What's the difference between the practice of the *puthujjana* and the *ariya*? Why are they different?

The *puthujjanas* are the ordinary riffraff, and the *ariyas* are the enlightened ones: the stream-winners, the once-returners, the nonreturners, and the arahants. *Puthujjana* actually means "ordinary person." That's why I call them the riffraff. A bit mean—I hope you don't mind.

One of the great sayings in the suttas is: "What the ariyas call happiness, the riffraff call suffering. What the ariyas call suffering, the riffraff call happiness" (Snp 762).

When you fall in love, "Oh, such happiness!" The whole world loves to love, but the ariya thinks: "Why are they doing that? That's going to be more suffering!" People who get married more than once think: "Oh, this time it's different. This is the real thing." They never learn.

Spending your holiday on meditation retreat, just sitting and sitting and sitting, hour after hour, sounds like suffering to some people. But those who understand Buddhism would say: "What happiness! What bliss!" People get it the wrong way round, and that's why the ariyas are sometimes totally misunderstood.

When I was an anagarika, people said to me, "What are you doing becoming an anagarika, spending your life as a monk?! You could do so much in this world. Get a wife, have kids. Are you afraid of relationships?"

I'm not afraid of relationships. The best relationship is the relationship with peace. The ariyas realize that simplicity, having few things, is much better than having a lot.

When I was in Hong Kong, I saw many Australians there shopping. And people from Hong Kong come to Perth and go shopping. There's something wrong with that, isn't there? I mean, Hong Kongers have shops in Hong Kong, and the Perthites certainly have shops in Perth. Why go to each other's cities to shop? It's crazy!

The ariyas would think: "Why do you go shopping? How much more do you need? How many pairs of shoes do you have to have? You've only got two feet; one shoe for each foot is enough. How many dresses do you need?" OK, maybe if you're twenty and you're looking for a partner—fair enough, get a few dresses if you're a girl; buy a few nice shirts if you're a guy. But then forget about it.

Forget about it and just wear your old clothes—they're much more comfortable. It's much worse being a woman than a man, as far as clothes are concerned, because women have to wear all these uncomfortable clothes. And high heels—I don't know how they manage that. It must be torture. They had this fashion once that the young women had to show their midriff. Their skirts or trousers were really low and the top part, which wasn't really a shirt, was up above the bellybutton. That might be OK in Singapore, but in Australia in the winter? I have seen young women who were blue in their midriff! I felt so much compassion for them. What young women have to do to get a partner! It's not worth it. Becoming a nun is much more sensible.

I'm not convinced that thinking has no value. I have yet to find a discourse by the Buddha that says, "Don't think, keep silent, be present, and that's enough for full realization." The first factor of the eightfold path is right view. When we totally denigrate thinking, isn't that how wrong view is perpetuated, with generations of Buddhists following blindly? Isn't that one of the main reasons behind the difficulties in reviving the bhikkhunī Sangha? Women were told for years that it's the way it is—don't think and be content. Is there a middle way? Silence is, of course, essential, but is it necessary to regard thinking as stupid and useless?

There are a couple of suttas that say one should let go of thinking, one of which is the *Dvedhāvitakka Sutta: The Two Kinds of Thought* (MN 19). In it the Buddha gives instructions on how to calm thoughts down. Right view is not the same as thinking. Right view is seeing clearly.

Imagine that I'm holding a stick and I ask you what it is. You might think I'm crazy asking you what a stick is, but eventually you'll say, "A stick." So then I'll ask you to be more descriptive, and you might tell me that it's brown, that it's made of wood.

That's thought, isn't it? You're thinking, but have you really seen the object yet? It's not a stick. It's not wood. It's not brown. It's much more than that. Our descriptions of things are limited. Thinking takes one aspect of reality and assumes that's all there is. You say it's a stick, and if I didn't ask you to elaborate, you'd stop there. That's the trouble with thought. It's an approximation and it never goes deep.

If you want to find out what something is, you've got to keep looking at it until all your thoughts—all these labels you've been taught—are exhausted. When you run out of labels, you start seeing what you haven't been taught, something much closer to reality.

Another problem with thinking is that it causes people to argue. Arguing is not a result of lack of thinking. Yet another problem with thinking is that it's bent—bent according to our conditioning. We all think in a certain way, and we're normally incapable of thinking outside the box. It's very difficult to think outside the box. It's easier for monks and nuns, because we live outside the box, apart from society. But everyone else is conditioned by TV, by education, by books, by monks, by any number of influences.

So how do we get out of this, this distorted way of thinking? The Buddha's teaching on the *vipallāsas* (distortions) is very beautiful (AN 4:49). How you think is based on your perceptions, and your perceptions are bent, or shaped, by your views. For example, if you believe in Christianity, or in Guan Yin (the goddess of mercy), or in the Pure Land, you will see the world according to your belief. There are many good people I know who swear they've seen Guan Yin. I remember a Vietnamese refugee girl who had escaped from communist Vietnam in a boat with others. They had been at sea for many days when they encountered a deadly storm. She swore to me that she saw Guan Yin coming across the water—absolutely clearly—and a few minutes later a British frigate appeared and took them all to Hong Kong.

If you have a certain view, it will create perceptions accordingly, and those perceptions will condition your thoughts. That's one of the reasons we have so many different religions and beliefs in the world, and why people are so sure of their beliefs that they will kill for them. They're absolutely sure, because they don't realize how uncertain thinking is. That's why some monks—some really good monks in Thailand and in England—are convinced that bhikkhunī ordination doesn't work. They have a view, and it conditions their perceptions. They're not even aware of perceptions that don't fit in with their views. A classic example is the difference between getting married and getting divorced. When you fall in love, the other person is beautiful and great. Because of your view, you actually perceive all these wonderful qualities in him or her, and you think how lucky you are to marry someone like that. But when you get divorced, your view is that the same person is a bastard. You're only able to perceive bad qualities: "It's obvious. Why didn't I see all that before?!"

It's exactly the same person. What has changed? Your whole framework of perception has flipped, and you can't see the good qualities anymore.

When you fall in love, you tell your mother and father, "I've met a wonderful girl." And when they say, "Don't marry her; you don't know her well enough," you will argue, "Oh, but she's beautiful, she's wonderful." You refuse to see anything bad about her. Even the way she picks her nose: "She's just so charming." When you want to see beauty, that's what you see.

That's the nature of our thoughts—they're bent.

When I first read that, it shook me. All my thoughts and views: how can I trust them if I know they're bent and distorted? Even your views about jhāna or about Buddhism—are they reliable? If you have the view that Buddhism is a good religion, you'll perceive good things in Buddhism. Then you'll think that Buddhism is a good religion, and that will reinforce your views. Views condition perceptions; perceptions condition thoughts; thoughts condition views. It's one of those vicious cycles. That's why you get trapped.

Buddhism teaches you to let go of thinking, to calm your mind, so that all the conditioning stops. You break the cycle. When you perceive without conditioning, everything that has been blocked out is there to be seen. The hindrances that stop you from seeing clearly are gone, especially the first two hindrances of desire and ill will. For the first time you don't deny what you don't like. Everything is very clear and true to reality. Only when you abandon your likes and dislikes, when you let go and become peaceful, can you trust what you see and perceive. As long as there's even a trace of like or dislike, the truth is bent. Your thinking will deceive you, life after life. That's why the Buddha described thoughts as being like the carcass of a dead dog hung around your neck (MN 20). That's the Buddha's teachings. I didn't make that up.

So be quiet and stop, and see what it's like. You'll know that the quiet mind has the taste of freedom, the *vimuttirasa*. You'll know that this is important, that it's beautiful and powerful. An incredible amount of wisdom arises from that silence.

I once heard that the best way to give back to your parents is through teaching the Dhamma. Please explain.

First of all, it's often difficult to teach your mother. I was a good teacher, but with my mother I gave up after a couple of years. Any other monk or nun could teach her, but not me.

According to the Pali commentaries, even Sāriputta, the wisest monk after the Buddha, was scolded by his mother. A few months before the Buddha passed away, Sāriputta went to visit his mother with some other monks. As soon as his mother saw him coming, she said: "You again! When are you going to get a proper job?" I don't know how old his mother was, but Sāriputta was eighty!

"So you want me to feed you again?" she said. "OK then, come inside."

But Sāriputta got such bad diarrhea that he died. Just before he did, a number of devas came to visit him. First one of the lower devas came, and there was a brilliant light in the room. His mother said, "Who was that?"

He said, "That was just a deva coming to pay respects to me."

"Oh, really?" she said.

Deva after deva came to visit him, each more powerful than the previous one, and the lights kept getting brighter. Eventually, Mahābrahma, the great god, came.

His mother said: "What was that? That was an incredible light in your room!"

"Oh, that's the god you worship all the time. He just came to say goodbye to me."

At that, she said, "Son, what have you been doing?"

Only then did she get faith, and he could finally teach her some Dhamma. Then he passed away.

You need the help of a few devas to convince your mother. Invite some heavenly beings along to impress her, and then maybe she'll listen. Remember, she has been teaching you since you were very tiny. You can't erase that relationship between mother and child: she'll probably see herself as your teacher for the rest of her life. That's just how it works.

The best way to teach your parents the Dhamma is to get them on a retreat. If you can convince them to do that, *and especially if you pay for it*, you've actually given them the gift of the Dhamma.

Dead Reckoning

If someone is dying, what should one do to ensure the best possible rebirth, or does it not matter too much? What advice do you have for people when they are about to die?

Dying is just like going to your final exam at university. What should you do just before you go in to take it? It's all a bit late to do anything at that point.

It's all the stuff you've done beforehand that really counts. If you want a good rebirth, live a good life. If you wait until the very end, it's usually too late.

There was a man from Singapore who was a so-called Vesak Buddhist because he went to the temple only once a year, for the Vesak celebration, and even then only because his wife forced him. He owned a shop and was more interested in making money than in going to the stupid temple. But to keep his wife quiet, he went there on Vesak days.

One year, as happened every year, he was getting bored, having to make donations and all that sort of stuff. He then heard a monk say that the most important thing before you die is your last thought. The monk also said that if you want to go to heaven, one of the best things to think of before you die is the Buddha, Dhamma, and Sangha—the Triple Gem. He asked the monk: "You mean I don't need to make any donations or keep precepts, I can have my whiskey every evening, go fishing, gamble, and have all the joys of life? All I need to do is think 'Buddha, Dhamma, Sangha' before I die?"

The monk said, "Actually, yes."

The man then thought of a way to ensure that his last thoughts would be "Buddha, Dhamma, Sangha." Because he had three sons, he decided to change their names to Buddha, Dhamma, and Sangha. When he died his children would be at his bedside, and he would say their names. Knowing that he was now safe, he stopped going to the temple: no more making donations, no more keeping precepts, just indulging himself.

Eventually the time came when he was on his deathbed and his three sons were next to him. His plan was working perfectly: "Buddha, Dhamma, Sangha, I'm going to heaven. Buddha, Dhamma, Sangha, I'm going to heaven."

Almost about to breathe his last breath, "Buddha, Dhamma, Sangha," he thought, "Hey, if my three sons are here, who's looking after my shop?" And that's when he died.

That old joke is a good story. It means that, yes, the last thought is important, but it's just one of many causes for your rebirth. Moreover, your last thought is the product of everything you've done in your life. If you've spent your life thinking about your business, that's what your last thought will be about. If you've spent your life thinking about cricket, your last thought will be about that. The only way to ensure a good rebirth is to live a good life. Your lifestyle determines your last thought.

Please tell us about dying the Buddhist way. Is it best to leave the dead person for several days?

Dr. Pim van Lommel, a cardiologist who wrote the fascinating book *Consciousness Beyond Life,* discovered that the stream of consciousness leaves when a person is brain-dead. In other words, when the brain stops working, you leave the body.

This means that you can do whatever you like with the body. You can take the organs out if you wish. I'm an organ donor. When I drop dead, take out all the organs you want, and then you can put the rest in the bin.

Buddhists should be organ donors! Some people say that if you give your eyes, you'll be blind when you go to heaven. No, you won't be blind: you'll get four eyes. No matter how many eyes you give, you get double that back in return. If you give your heart, you get two hearts. You never lose when you are generous and do charity.

When you're dead, you're dead. You don't have to leave the dead person for several days. That belief actually comes from the Tibetan tradition—it's in *The Tibetan Book of the Dead*, I think—which dates to well over a millennium after the Buddha. There's no such teaching in the original teachings of Buddhism. So just dispose of the body in the best possible way.

Even for the sky funerals in Tibet—putting the dead body outside to be eaten by vultures—it seems to be taken for granted that you don't have to wait. In fact, they used to do that in Thailand as well, in particular at the monastery where I ordained, Wat Saket, which is outside the old city walls of Bangkok. Wat Saket, the temple of the Golden Mount, was actually the cremation ground for most of Bangkok's population in the old days. I've seen a photo of a guy putting a body out with all the vultures waiting. I think we should go back to the old Thai tradition, instead of having these funerals that last for days and cost a lot of money. Anyway, the funeral was done almost immediately after the person died; they didn't wait for three or four or five days. So do whatever is necessary. You don't have to wait.

Sometime ago there was a myth going around in Malaysia and Singapore about where people go when they die. When a person is dying, you get monks or nuns to chant. Just as the person dies, you feel whether their head is hot or their feet are hot. If the feet are the last part of the body that's hot, it means that the person must have left his body through his feet and that he's going to a lower realm, which is bad. But if his head is the last part that's hot, then he has left his body through the top of his head, and it means he's going to heaven. Even people who knew their father was a scallywag, with a mistress here and a mistress there, would use this method to find out his future destination. When the head was the last part that was hot, the relations were so happy: "I don't know how your chanting could do this; it's a miracle. My father didn't deserve to go to heaven, but his head was the last part of his body to be hot!" The parents deserved to go down to the lower realms, but went to the higher realms instead because of the monks' chanting! And then they give huge donations to the monks.

But any doctor, or anyone who knows biology, knows that just before you die all the blood goes to the brain. The feet aren't important, but if your brain goes, you're in big trouble. It's the nature of the body to protect the brain as you die, and therefore all of the blood goes to the brain! That's an emergency response. So even for bad guys and gals, the head will always be the last part of the body to be warm. The monks are making money because of a myth. There's far too much superstition in this world, and sometimes people make money because other people are gullible.

When a Buddhist dies, just get rid of the body in the easiest possible way. Don't go around burning paper houses. All that does is produce smoke; nothing goes to heaven! The Hubble telescope has seen to the farthest reaches of our Milky Way galaxy and didn't see any devas up there. So where the heck does this smoke go? It doesn't even reach outer space! There's no one up there to receive it. So don't think that burning houses is going to make your father or mother get a house in heaven. Instead, if your parents are going to die, use that money to make some good kamma, and then share the merits. That does work. Please do something useful rather than waste money on burning paper.

What happens to a person who dies in jhāna? Does he or she get reborn with psychic abilities and an inclination toward meditation?

Number one, it's very difficult to die in jhāna. You may become invulnerable if you're in jhāna. There's one sutta and one personal anecdote that show what happens. The sutta is about two villagers who thought a monk in jhāna was dead (MN 50). Remember that when you're in jhāna, the body has totally vanished: you can't see or hear. If a doctor opened your eyelids and shone a light in your eyes, you wouldn't react. If the doctor shouted in your ear, you wouldn't hear anything. And you're not able to feel anything. This is what it's like in jhāna, and from the outside it looks like you're dead. The difference between being in jhāna and being dead is that in jhāna your body is still warm.

So, if any of you doctors out there find me in an emergency room or in a hospital bed, and you've been told I'm dead, be careful. If I'm warm, it's only jhāna. Then please send me back to the monastery. If I'm cold, send me down to the morgue. Don't mess up. If I come out of jhāna in the morgue, you may be responsible for the morgue attendants dying of heart attacks!

Back to the sutta. A monk is meditating in a forest, sitting in jhāna. Two villagers happen to walk by and see this monk who's not breathing. They think he's dead. Being Buddhists, they won't leave the monk to be eaten by jungle animals, so they give him a proper funeral. Since they're in the forest, they collect some wood, put the monk on top, light the fire, and leave. They don't hang around to watch him being cremated. You can imagine their surprise the next morning when that monk appears in the village on almsround and not even his robes are charred or burnt. According to this sutta, if you get into a deep jhāna, fire won't harm you or even the clothes you're wearing (MN 50).

The other story is a personal anecdote. There was an Indonesian monk I got to know many years ago. Sometimes you do meet people with psychic powers, real psychic powers. Such people are very rare and usually don't show them off, but if you're a monk you tend to find out. This monk got psychic powers from jhāna. At the time he was still a layperson living in Java. One day he went off into the jungle to live as a hermit. He told me that he saw a star (a nimitta) in his meditation and that he merged into this star. He didn't know how long he was merged with this star, but when he came out he noticed that the forest around him had changed. There had been lots of destruction, and he was partially submerged in water. He checked with the local villagers and discovered that for about six days there had been a flood. He had been totally submerged, to about twice his height. He hadn't known anything about it and was perfectly safe.

That's what happens in jhāna—you're perfectly safe. If people cremate you, your coffin will burn, but when they open the oven door, you'll come out just the same as you went in. And you'll still be wearing your robes!

What's the difference in mental condition at the time of death between those who have meditated and those who haven't?

The difference is in the wanting. If you meditate, you've conditioned yourself to let go of wanting. So at the time of death, there's a good chance that you'll be able to let go and become still. If you're perfectly still when you die, then when "they" come to take you to your next life, they won't see you, because you've disappeared. They'll go off without you. No more rebirth! But if you move, you've blown it—they'll see you and take you to your next destination.

Can you please explain the connection or disconnection between the brain and the mind?

That's a common question. Being a scientist, I have to quote the evidence, which comes from the work of researchers like Dr. John Lorber, a professor of neurology at Sheffield University who found a boy without a brain.

Professor Lorber was interested in the shape of the human skull. When he saw anyone at Sheffield University whose head was slightly misshapen, he invited that person to participate in his research. One day he noticed a postgraduate student with a slightly misshapen head. He was an honors graduate in mathematics. Professor Lorber gave the young man a CT scan and found that he had almost no brain! The area where most of his brain should have been was filled with cerebrospinal fluid. How to explain that the mind is a by-product of the brain when there is a brilliant mind and very little brain?

At a retreat I was leading in Sydney, a doctor told me he had seen that CT scan. He said the scan was done a couple of times just to make sure there was no error. He said that we wouldn't believe how many problems that one CT scan had caused for science, threatening billions of dollars of research. In the end, it was just filed away as an anomaly. In other words, it was just too difficult to explain and it challenged too many cherished opinions.

Other people have been discovered who have hardly any brain. The amount of brain they had could in no way explain their higher mental functions, such as memory or their ability to be honors students in mathematics.

Further evidence comes from Dr. Pim van Lommel (see also page 140), who did research on people with near-death experiences (NDE). These are people who have had some kind of trauma—an operation, an accident, or having to listen to one of my jokes—and as a consequence have had a cardiac arrest and an experience of leaving their body.

Van Lommel heard about people floating out of their bodies and being able to hear things. He decided to do research on whether what they heard was real or just imagined. His sample base was every cardiac-arrest patient who arrived at one of three hospitals over a certain period of time. He gave questionnaires to those who survived. At the same time, he recorded what was happening while they were in the emergency room or on the operating table. If they remembered any sounds or sights, he could then check to see if the memory was real. Of the huge number of people who took part in his research, about 10 percent had NDEs: what some of them said they had heard and seen while unconscious matched what had actually happened, so he had to conclude that these were real experiences.

His research became famous because those who had NDEs were also brain-dead—their brains were not functioning at that time. That was the crucial finding. Van Lommel realized that any conscious experience you have during an NDE—whatever you see and hear when you float out of your body—cannot have been produced by the brain. That was his great conclusion: consciousness must be a phenomenon separate from the brain.

That's very strong evidence that the mind doesn't depend on the brain. More evidence has been amassed since then, and it's pretty convincing these days.

What happens when you die?

When you die the mind starts to separate and become independent of the brain. It doesn't need the brain anymore. When it separates, that's when you get clarity. When you're dying, you're normally drugged up with morphine and other painkillers; your brain is really stuffed up. Also, during the dying process, all sorts of other stuff gets secreted into your brain, and so the brain is really malfunctioning at that time. But when the dying process gets to a certain point, the mind starts to separate, and that's when you can see, hear, and do things.

A classic case was related in an article in *Time* magazine by a doctor who had a patient with an inoperable brain tumor. He could see how the tumor was going to take over the brain of his patient, and he could predict what would happen. The patient gradually became paralyzed, lost his ability to speak, lost his memory, and then lost all the functions of the brain. The last part of the brain to function is the part that keeps the vital organs going, such as the heart and the lungs. Once there is no brain left to look after the heart and the lungs, you die. So the doctor was able to predict when his patient would die.

His whole family was present at his bedside. The patient had been in a coma for about a week. They were holding his hand, waiting for him to die. That's when he opened his eyes, sat up, and had a nice conversation with his family for about fifteen minutes. That shouldn't have been possible, but the doctor saw it with his own eyes. So for the last fifteen minutes of his life, when there was no brain activity left, the patient could again control his body. The mind takes over when you're very close to death.

Perhaps you're concerned about a family member who has dementia—please don't be. My mum had dementia for about three years before she died. I wasn't there when she died, but if I had been there when her mind separated from her brain, I'm sure she would have said: "Oh, Peter, how are you? How are things over in Australia?" She would have been totally aware, with all of her memory back.

Some people whose parents have dementia have told me that they've seen similar things. In the last moments of life, when the mind starts to separate from the brain, the brain malfunctions. But when the separation reaches a certain stage, the mind becomes clear again and memory returns.

We sometimes say that the last moments before you die are crucial for your rebirth. But you don't actually have to be afraid of taking morphine, thinking, "I'm going to be completely drugged to the eyeballs!" You don't need to worry about that, because in the last moments of the dying process your mind will naturally become clear.

The first time I read about the mind becoming clear right before death was in a short story by Tolstoy. He wrote about a guy who was so sick that he was screaming for hours every day, driving the people around him crazy. Some of them were trying to cure his constant pain, but others were losing it. Then, suddenly, he went quiet, and for five minutes he was totally clear, without any pain, and then he died. Tolstoy said this was a common occurrence in the days before morphine. No matter how much pain you're in or how sick you are, the last couple of minutes before you die you're totally pain-free and clear. That's good to know.

Two sisters were at the bedside of their father at Sir Charles Gairdner Hospital, in Perth, waiting for him to die. Suddenly he opened his eyes, sat up, and looked at his two daughters. Simultaneously, without any prior planning, they said, "We love you, Dad." Then he closed his eyes and died—another example of a clear mind during the last moment.

There was also a guy who was dying in the hospice at Murdoch University, in Perth. He had some kind of cancer and was drugged up to the eyeballs with morphine. He was from Yorkshire, a true Englishman. His daughter was a good Buddhist, and she had invited me to be there. It was getting time for my lunch, and so she went out to get some chicken and chips. Now, it's the custom for English people to share their chips. Though her dad was in a coma, she asked him out of habit, "Dad, do you want some chips?"

He came out of his coma and said, "Yes, please."

Those were his last words! He then went back into a coma and died soon afterward. A true Englishman!

During high states in meditation, such as jhāna, when you can no longer feel your body, breath, pulse, and so on, they are still detectable by a passerby, right? How can a meditator who has been in jhāna for hours, or days, return to the body if there's been no breathing, circulation, and so on? Wouldn't the physical body have ceased and started to decay well before the mind returned from its state of jhāna?

Even to a passerby, you're not breathing and there's no pulse when you're in jhāna. Here's the story of Greg. (See also the story of the forest monk on page 142.)

Greg usually meditated no more than half an hour or so. One Sunday afternoon, when there was nothing on TV, he told his wife he was going to his bedroom to meditate. When he hadn't returned after an hour and a half, his wife went to check on him. She found him in his bedroom, still sitting in meditation. He was perfectly still—too still!—his chest wasn't even moving.

She called 000 (the Emergency Call Service in Australia), and within five minutes the ambulance arrived. The medics rushed in. When they saw that Greg wasn't breathing, they felt for his pulse, but couldn't find it. They put him in the ambulance and turned the sirens on all the way to Sir Charles Gairdner Hospital. There was no pulse, no heartbeat, no nothing! In the emergency room he was given an ECG to measure his heart—the line was flat. To all appearances he was dead!

They measured his brain activity with an EEG—another flat line. He was brain-dead! He had cardiac arrest! His wife was terrified. She thought her husband had died.

Fortunately the doctor was of Indian descent! He had heard from his parents that you can suspend your life faculties in deep meditation, and now he was told by Greg's wife that Greg had been meditating. Perhaps this was a state of deep meditation.

The doctor put defibrillators on his chest and gave him electric shocks. Still, flat lines. For a long time the staff tried to resuscitate him, but nothing worked—until he came out of his meditation. He opened his eyes, sat up, and said: "What am I doing here? I was in my bedroom! What happened?" Meanwhile, as soon as he opened his eyes, the ECG and EEG started showing normal activity.

The doctor gave him a thorough examination and couldn't find anything wrong with him. So he let him walk home with his wife.

After he had told me the story, I asked him what he had done differently that time to get into such a deep jhāna. He said (and everyone says the same thing), "I really let go for the first time."

"How did you feel at the time?" I asked him. "Did you feel the defibrillators?"

"I couldn't feel anything," he said. "I was totally blissed out. It was the most wonderful experience I've ever had. It was so peaceful, so blissful."

That was hard evidence. Although he had defibrillators on his chest, he couldn't feel a thing, nor hear the sound of the ambulance's sirens. He had no idea what was going on. He was deep inside, having the time of his life!

That's a true story. Even passersby think you're dead!

The story shows you the difference between people in jhāna and those who are dead. One of the reasons the doctor used defibrillators on him was that his temperature was stable. This is described in the *Mahāvedalla Sutta* (MN 43), where it is said that the difference between a dead person and one in deep jhāna is that the body of the latter is still warm.

Q: Can laypeople get enlightened in this lifetime? If so, how do we do it?

A: Yes, you can. Just get lost!

Abbreviations

AN	Aṅguttara Nikāya
DN	Dīgha Nikāya
MN	Majjhima Nikāya
SN	Saṃyutta Nikāya
Ud	Udāna
Snp	Sutta Nipāta

For the Dīgha Nikāya, Majjhima Nikāya, Saṃyutta Nikāya, and Aṅguttara Nikāya, references are to the numbering scheme used in the English translations published by Wisdom Publications. For the Udāna and Sutta Nipāta, the numbering scheme used is that of the Pali texts published by the Pali Text Society.

Terms Explained

ahosi kamma: An action that is past, expired, or spent and will bear no further fruit or consequence.

ajahn: A Thai word that translates as "teacher," derived from the Pali word *ācariya*. It is a term of respect and is used as a title of address for Buddhist monastics.

anāgāmī: Nonreturner. A person who has abandoned the five lower fetters that bind the mind to the cycle of rebirth. After death he or she reappears in one of the *brahma* worlds called the pure abodes and attains *nibbāna* there.

anagarika: A person who has given up most or all of his or her worldly possessions and responsibilities to commit full-time to Buddhist practice. Anagarikas take on the eight precepts and usually wear white clothes or robes.

Anāgatavaṁsa: The chronicle of the future buddha Metteyya. A commentary and a sub-commentary of this chronicle describe future buddhas.

ānāpānasati: Mindfulness of breathing. A meditation practice of maintaining attention and mindfulness on the sensations of breathing.

anattā: Nonself, without soul. One of the three marks of existence shared by all sentient beings—namely, impermanence (*anicca*), suffering (*dukkha*), and nonself (*anattā*).

anicca: Not stable, not certain, impermanent. See *anattā*.

añjali: A gesture of respect used among Buddhists. It consists of putting one's palms together in front of the upper part of one's body.

Anuruddha: An eminent disciple of the Buddha's and his first cousin. In the suttas he is declared to be foremost among those with the divine eye.

Ālāra Kālāma and Uddaka Rāmaputta: The Buddha's two teachers before he left to practice on his own and became enlightened.

arahant (= Sanskrit *arhat*): A worthy one. A person who has achieved the highest stage of enlightenment.

ariya (= Sanskrit *ārya*): A noble one. A person who has attained one of the four stages of enlightenment.

Armadale: A suburb in Western Australia located on the southeastern edge of Perth's metropolitan area.

āsava: Outflowing, mental intoxication, or defilement; corruption of the mind.

avijjā: Delusion, illusion, ignorance, lack of understanding, especially in regard to the four noble truths.

avijjāsava: The corruption or outflowing of ignorance.

Bāhiya: An ascetic who was taught by the Buddha on the proper method of regarding all sense experiences. As he listened to the teaching, Bāhiya became an arahant. The Buddha declared Bāhiya to be foremost among those who swiftly comprehended the truth.

bhavāsava: The corruption or outflowing of existence. The craving to exist.

bhikkhunī: A fully ordained female monastic in a Buddhist tradition.

Bodh Gaya: The place where Buddha Gotama is said to have attained enlightenment.

Bodhinyana Monastery: A forest monastery in Serpentine, Western Australia, where Ajahn Brahm has been the abbot since 1995.

bodhisattva: In Mahayana Buddhism, a person who delays his or her attainment of nibbāna because of compassion for the suffering of beings. In Theravada, the person who was to become the Buddha.

***brahma* world**: A heavenly realm where *anāgāmīs* and those proficient in jhāna are reborn.

brahmavihāra: The four divine states of mind, the four noble sentiments, the four sublime abidings. They are *mettā* (loving-kindness), *karuṇā* (compassion), *muditā* (sympathetic joy), and *upekkhā* (equanimity).

Buddha Gotama: The historical Buddha, usually simply known as the Buddha.

Buddha Kassapa: The name of the third of the five buddhas of the present aeon, and the sixth of the six buddhas prior to the historical Buddha. These six are mentioned in the earlier parts of the Pali canon.

Buddhist holy sites: The sites of the Buddha's birth (Lumbinī), enlightenment (Bodh Gaya), first discourse (Sarnath), and death (Kusinārā).

buddho: Awakened, enlightened. A meditation mantra popularly used in the Thai forest tradition.

Chah, Ajahn (1918–92): A famous disciple of the Thai forest meditation master Ajahn Mun. Ajahn Brahm's teacher.

Cro-Magnon: Refers to the first premodern early humans of the European Upper Paleolithic. Currently the preferred term for them is European Early Modern Humans.

dāna: Gift, offering, alms.

deva: A heavenly being.

devī: A female heavenly being.

Dhamma (= Sanskrit *dharma*): The teachings of the Buddha.

Dhammananda, Dr. K. Sri (1919–2006): A highly respected Sri Lankan Buddhist monk and scholar.

Dhammasara Nuns' Monastery: A monastery for nuns (*bhikkhunīs*) in the forest tradition of Theravada Buddhism in Gidgegannup, outside Perth, Western Australia.

dukkha: Suffering. See *anattā*.

Edgar Allen Poe (1809–49): An American author, poet, editor, and literary critic.

eightfold path: The noble eightfold path, the *ariyo aṭṭhaṅgiko maggo*. One of the principal teachings of the Buddha, who described it as the way leading to the cessation of suffering and the realization of awakening.

ekaggatā: Unification of mind. A synonym for *samādhi*.

four noble truths: *Cattāri ariyasaccāni*. The central doctrine of Buddhism. It explains suffering (*dukkha*), its cause (*samudaya*), its cessation (*nirodha*), and the path leading to its cessation (*magga*).

Guan Yin: A female bodhisattva associated with compassion and venerated by many East Asian Buddhists. She is sometimes known as the goddess of mercy.

Hinayana: A term used historically by members of the Mahayana to refer to non-Mahayana schools of Buddhism. Since it means "lesser vehicle," is often construed as derogatory.

jackfruit: A species of tree native to parts of South and Southeast Asia. Its heartwood is used by Buddhist forest monastics in Southeast Asia to make dye, giving their robes their distinctive light-brown color.

Jagaro, Ajahn (b. 1948): An Australian disciple of Ajahn Chah and the first abbot of Bodhinyana Monastery.

Jains: Adherents of Jainism, an ancient religion from India that teaches that the way to liberation and bliss is to live a life of harmlessness and renunciation. Jainism and Buddhism existed side by side at the time of the Buddha.

jhāna: A meditative state of profound stillness in which the mind becomes fully immersed and absorbed in the chosen object of attention.

Jhana Grove: Jhana Grove Meditation Retreat Centre in Serpentine, Western Australia, established and managed by the Buddhist Society of Western Australia.

Jun, Ajahn (1922–95): A senior disciple of Ajahn Chah.

Kalimpong: A hill station in the Indian state of West Bengal.

kāmāsava: The corruption or outflowing of sensuality. Attachment to, and craving for, the five sense objects.

kamma (= Sanskrit *karma*): Action. An intentional choice that has future consequences.

karuṇā: Compassion, the second of the four sublime abidings.

kasiṇa: A class of visual objects of meditation. A *kasiṇa* meditation object is typically a colored disk.

khandha (= Sanskrit *skandha*): Aggregate. One of five groups of phenomena that constitute the essential aspects of human self-identity. They are: *rūpa* (form), *vedanā* (feeling), *saññā* (perception), *saṅkhārā* (volitional activities), and *viññāṇa* (consciousness).

khiḍḍāpadosika deva: Playful heavenly being.

loka-dhamma: Worldly matters or concerns that tend to preoccupy living beings. They are profit and loss, fame and dishonor, praise and blame, and happiness and unhappiness.

Maha Boowa, Ajahn (1913–2011): A famous disciple of the Thai forest meditation master Ajahn Mun.

Mahābrahma: A deity whose delusion leads him to regard himself as the all-powerful, all-seeing creator of the universe.

Mahāmoggallāna: One of the two chief disciples of the Buddha, the other being Sāriputta. Sāriputta and Mahāmoggallāna are declared to be the ideal disciples, whose example others should try to follow. Mahāmoggallāna's preeminence lay in his possession of psychic powers.

Mahābodhi Temple: A Buddhist temple at Bodh Gaya, marking the location where the Buddha is said to have attained enlightenment.

Mahayana: The "great vehicle." One of the three main classes of Buddhism, which spread north from India and now predominates in Tibet and East Asia.

mettā: Loving-kindness, goodwill, or benevolence. It is the first of the four *brahmavihāras*.

Metteyya or Maitreya: The name of the mythical next Buddha.

Mun, Ajahn (1870–1949): A founding master of the Thai Forest Tradition and teacher of Ajahn Chah.

muditā: Sympathetic joy or rejoicing in the good fortune of another. It is the third of the four *brahmavihāras*.

Namo Buddhāya: Homage to the Buddha. Used by many as a mantra in meditation.

nibbāna (= Sanskrit *nirvāṇa*): Extinguishment, cooling, emancipation, the highest happiness. *Nibbāna* refers to the extinguishment of desire (*lobha*), hate (*dosa*), and delusion (*moha*), and the end of suffering.

nimitta: Object of meditation, mark, sign. It is often used to refer to the mental image of a light, which is the result of deep meditation.

Nyanadhammo, Ajahn (b. 1955): An Australian disciple of Ajahn Chah.

Om maṇi padme hum: The mantra used by Tibetan Buddhists. *Maṇi* means "jewel" and *padma* "lotus flower." The lotus flower is a symbol of Buddhism.

paritta: Protection. The Buddhist practice of reciting certain verses and scriptures in order to ward off misfortune or danger.

Paṭācārā Bhikkhunī: A well-known bhikkhunī at the time of the Buddha and declared by him as foremost among the bhikkhunīs in Vinaya knowledge.

pīti: Joy, delight, rapture. *Pīti* is a specific joy associated with deep states of meditation.

pīti-sukha: Rapture and happiness. See *pīti* and *sukha*.

precepts: Buddhist code of ethical conduct. In Buddhism, the basic code of ethics is known as the five precepts. They are not formulated as imperatives but as training rules to be undertaken voluntarily.

There are other levels of precepts, namely the eight precepts, the ten precepts, and the *pātimokkha* (precepts for monks and nuns).

Pure Land: The celestial realm of a buddha or bodhisattva in Mahayana Buddhism. It also refers to a school of Buddhism.

puthujjana: An ordinary person, as opposed to a noble one (*ariya*).

Sakka: A heavenly being who is the ruler of Tāvatiṁsa heaven, according to Buddhist cosmology.

Sakyamuni: The Sage of the Sakyas. The Buddha was known by this name because he belonged to the Sakya clan.

samādhi: Mental stillness. The last factor of the noble eightfold path, composed of the four jhānas.

samatha: Calm. One of the main results of Buddhist practice. *Samatha* is usually paired with *vipassanā*, "clear seeing."

samsara: The cycle of death and rebirth, dictated by the laws of kamma. Release from this cycle comes only with the attainment of deep wisdom, or nibbāna.

Sangha: The Buddhist monastic community.

Sangharaja of Thailand: Sangharaja is the title given in many Theravada Buddhist countries to a senior monk who is the titular head either of a monastic fraternity (*nikāya*) or of the Sangha throughout that country. This term is often rendered in English as "Patriarch" or "Supreme Patriarch." The Sangharaja of Thailand mentioned on page 115 was Somdet Phra Nyanasamvara (1913–2013).

Sāriputta: One of the two chief disciples of Gotama Buddha, the other being his friend Mahāmoggallāna. In the suttas he is declared as foremost in wisdom in the bhikkhu Sangha.

Somdet Phra Buddhajahn (1928–2013): The abbot of Wat Saket Rajavaravihara (1971–2013) and an acting Sangharaja of Thailand (2005–13). He was Ajahn Brahm's preceptor.

Somdet Phra Nyanasamvara (1913–2013): Abbot of Wat Bovorn (1961–2013) and Sangharaja of Thailand (1989–2013).

stream-winner: *Sotāpanna*. One who has entered the stream of the eightfold path and is guaranteed to attain enlightenment in at most seven lifetimes. He or she has eradicated the first three fetters (*saṁyojanas*) of the mind. Stream-winning is the first of the four stages of enlightenment.

Sujato, Ajahn (b. 1966): An Australian Buddhist scholar and meditation teacher and a disciple of Ajahn Brahm.

sukha: Happiness, ease, pleasure, bliss. In a meditative context it refers to the deep sense of happiness that arises from deep meditation.

sutta (= Sanskrit *sūtra*): A discourse of the Buddha.

Tāvatiṁsa: The heavenly realm of the thirty-three gods, presided over by Sakka, a devotee of the Buddha.

Theragāthā: *Verses of the Elder Monks*. A work of 264 poems in the Pali canon in which the early monks recount their struggles and accomplishments along the road to becoming arahants.

Theravada: A term used for the type of Buddhism prevalent in Southeast Asia and Sri Lanka. It stresses the ideal of the arahant, as opposed to the Mahayana ideal of the bodhisattva.

Therīgāthā: *Verses of the Elder Nuns*. The work of seventy-three versified stories in the Pali canon in which the early nuns recount their struggles and accomplishments along the road to becoming arahants.

Triple Gem: The three refuges of a Buddhist: the Buddha, the Dhamma (the teachings), and the Sangha (the monastic community).

Tusita: One of the six heavens of the desire realm in Buddhist cosmology. It is where the Buddha is said to have resided before being reborn in the human realm to become enlightened.

upekkhā: Equanimity, evenness of mind. The detached state of one who witnesses without becoming emotionally involved. It is a virtue and an attitude to be cultivated, as opposed to simple indifference or lack of interest. It is the fourth of the *brahmavihāras*.

Vacchagotta: An ascetic (*paribbājaka*) whose conversations with the Buddha are depicted in the Pali canon. Vacchagotta eventually sought ordination from the Buddha and became an *arahant*.

Vajrayana: Buddhist tantra, which is a central feature of Tibetan Buddhism and some Buddhist sects in China and Japan.

Vesak: A Buddhist holy day celebrated on the full moon day of May in Theravada Buddhism. It commemorates the birth, enlightenment, and death of the Buddha.

vicāra: Examination, sustained application of mind. One of the mental factors present in the first jhāna.

vimuttirasa: The taste of liberation. All aspects of the Buddha's teachings are said to have this taste.

Vinaya: One of the three divisions of the Pali canon, comprising the monastic regulations.

vipallāsa: Distortion, perversion. There are three distortions: distortion of perception (*saññā-vipallāsa*), of consciousness (*citta-vipallāsa*), and of views (*diṭṭhi-vipallāsa*).

vipassanā: Clear seeing. Clear seeing of the three marks of existence: impermanence, suffering, and nonself. It is commonly used as a synonym for "vipassanā meditation."

vitakka: Thought, initial application of mind. One of mental factors present in the first jhāna.

Van Lommel, Pim (b. 1943): A Dutch cardiologist and scientist best known for his research on the subjects of near-death experiences and consciousness, including a prospective study published in the medical journal *The Lancet* on December 15, 2001.

Vulture Peak: One of the five hills encircling the city of Rājagaha. In the suttas, it is said that the Buddha visited it on several occasions and gave many of his discourses there.

Wat Bovorn: A temple in Bangkok and a center of the Dhammayut order, one of the two major monastic orders of Thai Buddhism. Prince Mongkut, who later became King Rama IV (page 115) was its first abbot.

Wat Pah Nanachat: The International Forest Monastery. A Buddhist monastery in northeast Thailand, established in 1975 by Ajahn Chah specifically as a training center for non-Thai monks.

Wat Saket: Wat Saket Rajavaravihara, The temple of the Golden Mount. A Buddhist temple in Bangkok. Ajahn Brahm was ordained at this temple with Somdet Phra Buddhajahn as his preceptor.

About Ajahn Brahm

AJAHN BRAHM was born in London in 1951. At age sixteen, after reading books on Buddhism, he began regarding himself as Buddhist, and his interest in Buddhism and meditation flourished while studying theoretical physics at Cambridge University.

He was ordained as a monk at age twenty-three and subsequently spent nine years studying and training in the forest meditation tradition under the renowned meditation master Venerable Ajahn Chah.

In 1983 he was invited to go to Australia to help establish a forest monastery near Perth. Ajahn Brahm is now the abbot of Bodhinyana Monastery and the spiritual director of the Buddhist Society of Western Australia.

In 2004 Ajahn Brahm was awarded the prestigious John Curtin Medal for vision, leadership, and community services.

In 2005 Ajahn Brahm started a project to build a mediation center that provides a suitable environment for laypeople to receive training in meditation. Jhana Grove was inaugurated in April 2009. Since then, a large number of meditation retreats have been held there every year.

A highly sought after speaker around the world, Ajahn Brahm attracts thousands to his inventive and insightful talks.

Also Available from Ajahn Brahm

Kindfulness

"In a stroke of genius, Ajahn Brahm turns mindfulness into kindfulness, a practice that opens our hearts to others as well as to ourselves." —Toni Bernhard, author of *How to Be Sick*

Don't Worry, Be Grumpy
Inspiring Stories for Making the Most of Each Moment

"If a picture is worth a thousand words, then a good metaphorical story is worth that many more. Ajahn Brahm's latest collection of stories is funny, endearing, and, of course, infused with wisdom."—Arnie Kozak, author of *Wild Chickens and Petty Tyrants*

Who Ordered This Truckload of Dung?
Inspiring Stories for Welcoming Life's Difficulties

"Ajahn Brahm is the Seinfeld of Buddhism."—Sumi Loundon Kim, author of *Blue Jean Buddha*

Mindfulness, Bliss, and Beyond
A Meditator's Handbook
Foreword by Jack Kornfield

"Riveting and real. I can't tell you how thrilled I was to read it."—Glenn Wallis, translator of *The Dhammapada: Verses on the Way*

The Art of Disappearing
The Buddha's Path to Lasting Joy

"In this well-done and illuminating work, Brahm shines a light on the spiritual practice of mindfulness."—*Spirituality & Practice*

About Wisdom Publications

Wisdom Publications is the leading publisher of classic and contemporary Buddhist books and practical works on mindfulness. To learn more about us or to explore our other books, please visit our website at wisdompubs.org or contact us at the address below.

Wisdom Publications
199 Elm Street
Somerville, MA 02144 USA

We are a 501(c)(3) organization, and donations in support of our mission are tax deductible.

Wisdom Publications is affiliated with the Foundation for the Preservation of the Mahayana Tradition (FPMT).